W9-DBX-025

# SPEAKING

## to

# INFLUENCE

# SPEAKING
## to
# INFLUENCE

*Mastering Your Leadership Voice*

Laura Sicola, PhD

**All rights reserved.**

Copyright © 2019 by Laura Sicola

No part of this book may be reproduced or transmitted in any form or any means, electronic or mechanical, including photocopying, recording, or by any information storage or retrieval system, without permission in writing from the Publisher.

**Copyright Notice**

Publisher: Jesse Krieger

Write to Jesse@JesseKrieger.com if you are interested in publishing through Lifestyle Entrepreneurs Press

Publications or foreign rights acquisitions of our catalogue books.
To learn more about our publications or to acquire foreign rights for our catalogue books, visit: www.LifestyleEntrepreneursPress.com

Any unauthorized use, sharing, reproduction or distribution of these materials by any means, electronic, mechanical, or otherwise, is strictly prohibited. No portion of these materials may be reproduced in any manner whatsoever, without the express written consent of the publisher.

ISBN: 9781948787307

# Praise for
# *Speaking to Influence:*
# *Mastering Your Leadership Voice*

Dr. Sicola reminds us that if we want to lead, we must focus every day on the how and the what of communicating. *Speaking to Influence* is a must-read for anyone serious about making an impact and a difference.

*– Christopher Caine, President and CEO, Mercator XXI, LLC*

I've watched Laura work and prepare clients for media appearances on camera, on stage, and in the boardroom, and I can tell you the skills and principles she teaches make all the difference.

*– Lu Ann Cahn, 8-time* Emmy-award-winning *journalist, professional speaker, author, Director of Career Services, Klein College of Media and Communication at Temple University*

*Speaking to Influence* spoke volumes to me. I could not help thinking about our need to navigate our complex world, work, and everyday lives. Influencing is a large part of what we do every day. *Speaking to Influence* is the go-to book for anyone who desires to control what can be controlled and to influence what cannot.

*– Angelo Valletta, President and CEO - The Catholic Foundation of Greater Philadelphia*

We consistently rely on Laura's expertise to improve the leadership communication skills of our Fellows. She never disappoints. Our Fellows leave prepared to communicate clearly and effectively in their roles around the world. *Speaking to Influence* is a great resource for anyone who wants easy access to her guidance right at their fingertips.

*– Tamara Fleming, EdD, Executive Director, Longwood Fellows Program, Longwood Gardens*

Dr. Laura Sicola has been a guest on my show a number of times, and with each visit you can see why Fortune 500 companies call upon her to teach their executives how to become more effective leaders. She practices everything she preaches. Dr. Sicola's new book *Speaking to Influence: Mastering Your Leadership Voice* gives you all the tools you need to be on top of your game.

— *Gary Alan, Host of The Express radio show*

To my sons, Thomas and Dante. May they grow to be examples of the kind of inspirational leadership necessary to make the world a better place.

Image consultants often say that people make their initial judgment
of you within the first seven seconds of meeting you.
I say the next seven seconds matter even more,
because that's when you open your mouth and
prove whether or not their first instinct was correct.

# TABLE OF CONTENTS

# FIGURES AND TABLES LIST

# SPEAKING
## to
# INFLUENCE

# PREFACE

*'In that direction,' the Cat said, waving its right paw round, 'lives a Hatter: and in that direction,' waving the other paw, 'lives a March Hare. Visit either you like: They're both mad.'*
*'But I don't want to go among mad people,' Alice remarked.*
*'Oh, you can't help that,' said the Cat: 'we're all mad here. I'm mad. You're mad.'*
*'How do you know I'm mad?' said Alice.*
*'You must be,' said the Cat, 'or you wouldn't have come here.'*
—Lewis Carroll. *Alice's Adventures in Wonderland.*

One of the most maddening experiences is when you make a seemingly simple point in conversation, only to have it escalate into a mind-boggling maze of misinterpretations, clarifications, ruffled feathers, debate, embarrassment, circular arguments, or worse. Perhaps equally frustrating is to make a great point, only to have it fall on deaf ears. It gets glossed over, as if you had never said it in the first place—or worse, the response is as if you weren't even there in the room. Either way, you know that you are not making the impact you want to make, if you are indeed making any impact at all.

It's during these moments that your instinctive reflex is to blame the other person, and ask yourself, "What's wrong with them? Why don't they understand what I mean? Why can't they see that I'm right, how important this issue is, and how great my idea is?"

It's easy to feel like you've entered some fictional world like Lewis Carroll's Wonderland, where everyone is mad (in the sense of crazy, not angry—although that's often the case as well). And once you've had enough of these conversations, you may start to believe that the Cat's final assessment might be right after all: you must be mad too, otherwise, why would your conversations keep following the same patterns?

That's why, in attempt to keep a bit of humor within the context of discussing an incredibly important topic—influential leadership communication—each chapter in this book begins with a quotation from Carroll's *Alice's Adventures in Wonderland* or *Through the Looking Glass*. Carroll's masterful word play allows his characters to unabashedly and unapologetically break all sorts of rules regarding everything from simple manners and social etiquette to sports matches and courtroom procedures.

In reading the stories in general and the selected quotes in particular, it's easy to appreciate the cleverness in the way the Mad Hatter, the Caterpillar, the Cheshire Cat, and others twist Alice's words around and challenge her assumptions about what is normal, good, and right. It can be rather sobering, however, when similarly unprovoked challenges come our way.

With that, I invite you to join me and take a tumble down the dark rabbit hole as we explore what creates that sense of madness when we interact with others, regardless of the context. While I can't promise that you'll wake up to realize it was all a dream, as Alice did, I can promise to share with you the tools necessary to help you make sense of the madness and find your way to the clarity of daylight.

# ACKNOWLEDGEMENTS

There are so many people without whose help and support this book would not have been possible. As I initially sat to write this, a fleeting concern was that some of it would sound repetitive, like the acknowledgements I've made in earlier works. Then I realized how beautiful that is: to have a core group of people who continue to inspire, love, and support me, in addition to the wonderful new additions who have more recently entered my life. It is an honor and a pleasure to recognize them here.

First, I am continually grateful to my family: To my husband, Larry, for being my greatest fan and advocate; my parents, Tom and Nadine, for being excited for me with every milestone; and my sons, Thomas and Dante, who give my work purpose, challenge me to put my money where my mouth is as a teacher and communications professional, and make my heart smile every time they enter the room.

I am grateful to and humbled each day by my clients and graduate students, all unique in their personal and professional goals and challenges, who have invited me on their journeys and allow me to be a part of their transformations into the leaders and role models they aspire to be. May they learn even half as much from me as I learn from them.

JV Crum III, founder and CEO of Conscious Millionaire and my long-time business coach, and Karen Hawthorne, the integrator to my visionary, not only have pushed me to see the bigger potential in my business itself, but have helped me develop the blueprints and take the steps to build it.

Chris Caine, president and CEO of Mercator XXI, was the first to see the value of my skill set as essential in the business world and introduce me to the world of consulting and entrepreneurship. And Grace Killelea, founder and CEO of The GKC Group, was the first to recognize and validate my niche in vocal executive presence as "a game changer."

And last but not least, special thanks to Jesse Krieger and his team at Lifestyle Entrepreneurs Press: COO Kristen Wise, marketing director Maíra

Pedreira, and my editor, Michael Ireland, who maintained an impressive balance of diplomacy and moral support along with an eagle-eye for detail while holding my feet to the fire as we got down to the wire. Without all of them, this book would still be a half-written draft in bits and pieces somewhere in my hard drive.

Each of you has encouraged me to take another leap of faith to a make an ever-greater, positive impact on the world. Until we take the first leap, it is not possible to soar...

# INTRODUCTION

You're an expert in your field. You know your material inside and out and can recite key statistics in your sleep. There's no one more qualified than you to be in your position, and if you're not already at the top, you should be, *BUT...*

*It's always the "but."* It's the "but" that always indicates there is a critical imbalance between your technical expertise and your soft skills. More specifically, the way you communicate, especially in critical moments, seems to miss the mark. Maybe:

- you don't captivate people's attention when standing at the front of a room
- you don't project (or feel) authority and confidence
- you're good at working with people in your department but can't seem to get your point across effectively to people in other departments
- people don't seem to listen to you when you talk, or you don't feel like you get the respect you deserve
- you freeze when put on the spot, or get defensive when your fight-or-flight reflex kicks in
- you should be the one who gives the conference presentations and media interviews but you don't know how to tell a good story or panic at the idea of being on stage or on camera
- you don't handle conflict skillfully, either avoiding it at all costs or burning bridges, perhaps even unbeknownst to you, or
- you tend to get "lost in the weeds" instead of being concise and getting right to the heart of what the audience wants to know and why.

These are just some of the common lamentations I hear from people who realize there is a knowledge and skills gap keeping them from being the inspirational leader they *know* they can be, and having the impact they want.

If any of these challenges sounds familiar, this book is for you.

Having technical expertise in finance, engineering, marketing, pharmaceutical research, or any other area is terrific, and will get you the reputation of being an expert. But at some point in your career you will hit a plateau, because being an expert isn't enough to be recognized as a true *leader*. Even if you *do* manage to rise to a top position, you'll recognize, deep down, that you're not having the right effect, or getting the results you want...as leadership coach Marshall Goldsmith wisely said in the title of his book, *what got you here won't get you there*.

You need to balance that expertise with the ability to communicate so effectively that you can get through to just about anyone, anywhere. You know you have to capture their attention, help them relate to you and see the importance of the scenario you are describing. You have to get them on board, inspired by and committed to working with you to see the plan through.

"Is that even possible?" you may wonder. It may seem like a nice ideal, but not a realistic goal. I'm here to tell you it is not only possible, but it is achievable—with the right tools and understanding and a little bit of practice. I'll provide the tools and understanding; the last piece will be up to you. Ask yourself: *"Am I committed to ensuring that when I talk, people see an inspiring leader?"*

Whether you're speaking in a meeting, on a conference call, on stage, on television, in a webinar, or anywhere else, the way you present yourself and your message makes the difference between whether or not people follow because they *have* to, or because they *want* to. In that distinction lies the difference between whether you lead an initiative that lasts a season, or create a legacy that lasts a lifetime.

Join me on this journey to discover your untapped powers of speaking and influence.

# CHAPTER 1

## LEADERSHIP AND INFLUENCE

---

*'Would you tell me, please, which way I ought to go from here?'*
*'That depends a good deal on where you want to get to,' said the Cat.*
*'I don't much care where—' said Alice.*
*'Then it doesn't matter which way you go,' said the Cat.*
*'—so long as I get SOMEWHERE,' Alice added as an explanation.*
*'Oh, you're sure to do that,' said the Cat, 'if you only walk*
*long enough.'*
—Lewis Carroll. *Alice's Adventures in Wonderland.*

---

## I.  INTRODUCTION

At some point or other, consciously or unconsciously, we all are like Alice, uncertain of our purpose, direction, or goal. Whether it pertains to something as big as our career path or the vision for our company, or as small as what we want to get out of participating in a conference call, we go through the motions without really thinking about how to get the greatest value out of the experience.

People who report to you may take Alice's role occasionally: They just want direction. At this point, hopefully you're more helpful than the Cheshire Cat, who provided no useful guidance at all.

The bigger challenge, however, is when you DO know where you want to go, but can't seem to get others to join you on the journey. At that point, it's time for a little critical self-analysis, so, ask yourself: "Do I come across as a leader with a message worth hearing and a vision worth pursuing?"

## II.  THE PERCEPTION OF LEADERSHIP

Did you notice I did not say you should ask yourself if you *are* a leader with a compelling message and vision? The question is whether or not you are *seen* as one, regardless of how competent and confident you feel inside.

Have you ever wondered how some people always manage to be persuasive, compelling, and influential? Why do some people's voices always seem to be heard, regardless of their volume? How do you get the right person's ear, and get them to hear not just what you have to say, but to hear *you?* That means not just that they hear you passively, but that they listen consciously to what you are saying, process it, understand both your content and your *intent*, and ultimately get on board with your vision. That's what this chapter is going to look at. The irony of it all is that when you think about it, leadership is an *image*, not an official job title or role. After all, do you know anyone whose business card has their title listed as "leader?" Neither do I.

**Leadership is an *image*.**

People follow "the person in charge" because they *have to*; that's implied in their job description. In contrast, they follow someone they *perceive* as a "leader" because they *want* to. It's a matter of trust, integrity, reputation... and whether or not others understand and appreciate where you are trying to lead them!

Whether it's your vision for something as small as what you want to accomplish in a meeting, the legacy you want to establish for yourself, or where you want to take the company over the next decade, you need to be clear on two things:

- you need to understand exactly what you want that outcome to look like, and
- you need to articulate your vision to others in a way that gets through to their minds and hearts (and sometimes, their wallets!).

Before we jump into how to achieve clarity on these two objectives, let's clear up a few common points of confusion.

## III. PERSUASION, MANIPULATION, AND INFLUENCE: KEY DISTINCTIONS

Many people get stuck and end up sabotaging their powers of influence because they conflate the concept of "influence" with "persuasion" and "manipulation." Naturally, there is some overlap in desired outcomes for each, but if you want to reach your fullest potential as a communicator and leader, it's critical to recognize the difference.

### A. Persuasion

Persuasion is a conscious, active effort that ultimately boils down to getting someone to agree to your specific, desired outcome. It's about convincing people to come to your side, whether you use a logical argument, a carrot-or-stick incentive, or an appeal to their emotions (for example).

For instance:

- if I as a supervisor need you to do a last-minute push for an ambitious sales goal, which would require a lot of late nights, but I offer you an extra bonus if you meet the goal, I will probably be able to persuade you to accept the challenge, assuming the size of the bonus "carrot" is sufficiently motivating, or

- if I (again as a supervisor) remind you gently that budgets have been strained lately and there have been talks of layoffs in the near future if the team doesn't make quota, this "stick" might be equally persuasive in motivating you to try to reach that sales goal, or

- if I as your employee strike up a conversation with you about a photo of your family on your desk, and get us to bond for a moment about some laughable moments of parenthood before I ask you for an afternoon off at an inconvenient time so I can catch my child's dance recital, it may be easier to persuade you to grant my request.

I was once planning a major event to be held in October, when a client in the agribusiness world commented, "Oh, I'd love to send my whole staff, but that's right in the middle of potato-harvest season, and they'll kill me if I add one more thing to their calendars!" Knowing that several of the other clients I wanted to invite were also part of that industry, I moved the event to mid-

November. Although she wasn't overtly trying to get me to change the date, the evidence she offered persuaded me to do so.

## B. Manipulation

Manipulation tends to have a negative, dishonest, or even underhanded feeling to it. Whether done overtly, covertly, or passive-aggressively, manipulation is about forcing someone to do what you want, typically when it goes directly against what they want, and it disregards their feelings, needs, or other reasoning.

In the movie *The Wolf of Wall Street*, Leonardo DiCaprio played a master manipulator, institutionalizing a strategy for lying to prospective clients about investment opportunities to trick them into investing far more than they could afford or felt comfortable spending. When on the phone with male prospects who claimed they wanted to check with their wives before buying anything, he would subtly challenge their manhood, telling them they shouldn't need their wives' permission to spend money that they (the men) had earned. He knew that for every dollar they lost, he would gain personally, and that's all he cared about, so he pressured them until they gave in and gave him their money.

Then again, manipulation need not be so sinister. My five-year-old niece, Michala, for example, is a master manipulator. At the end of a family holiday gathering, when her parents tell her it's time to stop playing and go to bed, she'll go around the room hugging and kissing people, saying, "I love you!" and continuing conversations with each of them. Upon second and third reminders that it's bedtime, she protests, "But I'm just telling Aunt Laura that I love her and I'll miss her." The more her parents try to coax and persuade her to go, the more she turns up the charm. She's not fooling anyone, of course, but she knows perfectly well that the sweet smile, big blue eyes, and loving words of affection to everyone in the room make it hard to reprimand her or get (at least publicly) angry with her, providing a great stall tactic that can delay bedtime for an impressive length of time.

## C. Influence

Influence, in contrast, is a power that goes way beyond an immediate conversation or decision. It certainly includes the skills of persuasion, to be used as necessary, but the beauty of true influence is that you don't need to be present for others to see its effects.

> *A few years ago, I was teaching graduate courses part-time at the University of Pennsylvania, while building my consulting practice. I often hired my former graduate students as project interns. One year, when I offered the position to Allison,[1] a recent student, I suggested she speak with Diana, one of the prior year's interns to get the "inside scoop" on what it was like. Ultimately Allison accepted the position, and later she shared with me that the input she had received from Diana was, "It's fun, but it's a lot of work. When project deadlines draw near, you can expect to have some nights when you're up until 2:00 a.m. trying to get everything done. But the thing is, Laura will be right there with you until it's finished." And that was what convinced her to take the position. I had nothing to do with the conversation that ultimately persuaded her to join the team, but the impact of how I ran my company and my team created a reputation that influenced someone's decision and the outcome of my project.*

Your leadership style could motivate an employee, out of loyalty to you and a commitment to your company's mission, to turn down another job an executive recruiter offers them, or it could convince her to jump ship at the first opportunity to find greener pastures. Either way, you may never know what occurred. That's the power of influence.

Influence also has a ripple effect. During an annual review, a manager may give an employee constructive feedback with diplomacy, tact, and respect, leaving the employee feeling clear on his objectives and motivated to perform better, because that is how the manager has always received feedback from you as *their* boss. That is most certainly evidence of your

---

[1] All names used in the examples, anecdotes, and personal stories in this book have been changed, unless the persons mentioned have given me explicit permission to use their real names. I am grateful to all my clients, colleagues, and loved ones for the opportunity to use their learning experiences in this book.

influence and it is the kind of influence you want to have. There are times when you will win and times you will lose an argument, times when you will persuade someone to accept your view, and times when others will persuade you. But in the end, you want to know that your leadership style ensures that you get the respect you deserve and always has a positive effect on the outcome. One of the primary factors that determines this is how you communicate.

## D.  Communication and Leadership

Ultimately, the way you speak as a leader *will* have one of two possible effects: It will convince others to join you, or it will convince them *not* to. For example, beware:

- If your contributions are so technical that people can't follow them, they will lose interest.
- If you deliver your information dryly, it may seem like you don't care, or like you don't feel it matters.
- If you seem nervous or unconfident when speaking, people will doubt your expertise and credibility.
- If you are overbearing in asserting your opinion, people will avoid engaging in discussion with you at all, and resist before inviting you to join a team.

On the other hand, you can create a magnetism that compels people to pay attention and get on board:

- If you explain things in a way that makes sense to the audience,[2] it's easy for them to see your perspective.
- If you make them feel respected and valued, they will be much more motivated to partner with you.

---

[2] In this book, I use the term audience broadly, to mean the intended recipient of your message, in any context. Whether your audience is in a traditional "audience" setting as you give a formal presentation, or just listening to you over the telephone, reading an email you sent, or watching your facial expressions change as you listen to them talk, you are communicating something to them. The issue at hand is what message they are receiving, and whether or not it is the one you want to send.

> ▓ If you show the right level of confident, positive enthusiasm in making your point, they will be more likely to trust that what you are saying is correct.

Simply put, if you want to get out of your own way and gain (or regain) control of your future as a true leader, you have to build a following. A "following" is not just a bunch of people below you on the company org chart, but is instead a group of people who understand your vision and are loyally committed to you, to each other, and to seeing that vision become their reality. This includes employees, bosses, board members, clients, and vendors (to name just a few). You also need to create a culture and environment that reinforces and supports people in their individual and collective efforts to promote that outcome.

## E.  Culture

Organizational culture doesn't come about as a result of writing policy or having staff memorize the company handbook. Regardless of what your company handbook claims, culture is learned and spread through a type of "osmosis."

What I mean by this is that, for example, when you speak to people in any context, your voice fills the air and surrounds them. Those listening will absorb some or all of your message, depending on a variety of factors ranging from how diplomatic you are, your facial expressions, your efforts to listen, the examples you use or omit, your tone of voice, and more. More importantly, with that message, they will also absorb an understanding of what kind of communication style you value. By extension, they will infer what they think you believe leadership communication sounds like, and what speaking style the company values, and they will pass it along to others in the same way—for better or worse.

Alternatively, listeners may reject your leadership and your message, resist change, and perhaps even resent the situation, all of which leads to the creation of a completely different kind of culture. In that context, you are a leader in name and rank only...you have no true followers...and that eats away at the root of the culture you are trying to establish.

You may have knowledge, expertise, insights, and experience, along with an incredible vision of a future you believe to be possible for yourself, the company, or both. To achieve that vision, however, you need to get buy-in, which requires getting others to be as enthusiastic as you are—by seeing how their own roles and efforts can contribute to that vision becoming a reality.

## F.   Challenges

It may sound a bit ominous, but what it all boils down to is that no matter how good your technical expertise is, that's not enough to get to—and succeed at—the top. What obstacles do you face?

- Maybe you're frustrated because you want to take the company in a new direction. You need to minimize resistance and get everyone on board. When you speak, people *seem* to listen but they don't "get it." They might go along with it, but their hearts aren't in it. You don't want to be constantly arguing with people, but you don't want "yes-men" either.
- Maybe you're at the top of the corporate ladder (or at least pretty high up) and oversee teams across functions and cultures, and it is your responsibility to get them all to work together collaboratively and productively...which is easier said than done, especially if you're someone whose fight-or-flight reflex goes into overdrive at the slightest hint of conflict.
- Maybe you're not at the top *yet*, but you want your boss to realize unequivocally that you are the next obvious person for that big promotion.
- Maybe you suddenly need to be the public "face" of the organization, speaking at conferences, on promotional videos, client events, perhaps even giving a TED talk, and you need your natural charisma to shine through with confidence and polish.
- Maybe you lack the confidence to say what you really want to say in front of the right people, or you have a lot of information to share and stories to tell but you don't know how to do it in a way your target audience will find interesting.
- Maybe you know your product and company inside and out, but also know that you'd close more deals if you could connect better with prospective customers, board members, or investors.
- Or, maybe you lead or attend lots of meetings but feel like people don't listen to you, or simply aren't engaged when you talk.

If you find yourself nodding your head knowingly at one or more of these scenarios, keep reading, because this book is for you.

## G.  What This Book Is NOT

One concern I hear often from people is that they feel uncomfortable and "fake" when they try to modify the way they talk in order to become a more effective speaker. While we'll address these issues throughout this book, I'm not going to teach you how to act—I couldn't even if I wanted to. I'm not an actor or a singer. Trust me, if you hand me a script from Shakespeare, nobody will be happy with the result. And beyond singing in a church choir and the occasional karaoke night (I lived in Japan for several years; it's practically a religion there), you won't find me performing major works of art—it's enough of a stretch for me to refer to karaoke and "art" in the same sentence.

My training is not from the theater or performing arts world so you never have to worry about feeling like I'm trying to turn you into someone you're not. Unless, that is, I'm helping you become the person you genuinely *want* to be.

As a result, this book is not full of scripts, lists of decontextualized vocal exercises, blocking techniques, strategies for memorizing a script, or instructions for when to use which hand gestures in a speech.

Similarly, you will not find lots of questions exploring your psychological history, or other theoretical analyses, nor will you find a lot of technical medical descriptions of the mind or body. I am neither a psychologist nor a speech pathologist. I'm not that kind of doctor, and frankly, I'm not going to "fix" or "heal" you because you're not broken or sick.

That being said, many clients have told me happily that the discoveries they have made while working with me were "cathartic," "liberating," and "therapeutic." Others have said working together was "better than therapy."

## H.  What This Book IS

I am a linguist, so my work stems from an in-depth understanding of three areas:

- first, the nuances of the English language itself (and a few others),
- second, how the mind processes speech, and

■ third, the kinds of social, psychological, cultural, or other contextual factors that influence how speech is expressed and interpreted (or misinterpreted).

My approach focuses on putting these factors together to understand the impact your communication style is having on your success as a leader and influencer.

## 1. Identifying Your Blind Spot

One universal blind spot we all have to one extent or another is in our understanding of the critical and defining gap between:

■ how we *want* to come across to others when we speak,
■ how we *think* we come across, and
■ how we *actually* come across.

The first is the way you want to be seen, your desired image and reputation— what the Cheshire Cat might otherwise identify as *where you want to go*. You need to be honest with yourself and acknowledge how it does or does not match up with the impression you believe you make, i.e., *where you think you are* and *how far you think you have to go to reach your destination*. Then, what is most important for growth and success is to compare those views with your current image and reputation, i.e., *where you actually are now*, to identify where there's a disconnect between the ideal impact you want to have and the reality of the impact you're having currently.

We tend to be oblivious to this last point. Need proof that this claim applies to you? How often have you watched yourself in a video made only seconds before, and thought to yourself, "Oh my gosh, that sounded so much better in my head!" "What was I doing with my hands there?" or, "That's so weird, why do I look angry?" If you're like most people, you know *exactly* what I'm referring to here.

If you sincerely want to identify your blind spot in order to get unstuck and make progress toward establishing your ideal reputation as a leader, start asking a *wide variety* of people to share what they see as your strengths and weaknesses, whether pertaining to your role or otherwise. Even—and *especially*—if you hear something you don't like, *thank* them for their honesty, and *treat that information like gold*. Those are people you know you can trust, and whose input will help you reach your goals, if you act on it correctly. You can start by mapping out your goals and findings in the following diagram.

## 2.   *Mapping Out Your Image and Reputation Goals*

**Figure 1: Identifying Your Desired Image and Reputation**

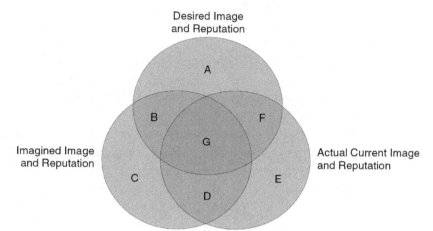

In Figure 1, we see your three images of yourself: desired, imagined, and actual. They overlap as follows:

- ▧ Section A represents your Goal: These are qualities you want people to see in you, but they don't right now, and you're clear on that.
- ▧ Section B holds delusions and wishful thinking: These are positive qualities you *think* others already see in you, but they do not. This is in your blind spot.
- ▧ Section C is also in the blind spot, but would be a relief for you to discover. It holds your concerns that you have a negative reputation for something, but in fact you do not. Take comfort in discovering this part of your blind spot.
- ▧ Section D identifies the areas in which you already *know* you don't have the best reputation. You know you need to fix it, and this area should be a top priority to address. This Section goes along with Section A, confirming what you know you need to change.

13

- Section E is the Danger Zone in your blind spot: These are qualities you do *not* want people to associate with you, *but they do, and you don't realize it*. Seeking feedback proactively, sincerely, and humbly to identify what is in this space is paramount to getting you unstuck and heading in the right direction. This goes together with Section B as the hardest sections to identify because they reflect areas in which your perception of your own image is more inflated than how others see you. Accepting reality is both unpleasant and humbling, which often inspires resistance and denial, the kiss of death for true growth.

- Section F is a pleasant surprise: You want people to recognize these characteristics in you, and they do, but you didn't *realize* it. Take comfort and gain confidence in this new knowledge. This is the flip-side to Section C.

- Section G is the proverbial brass ring: This is the point at which you are confident in your knowledge that you are projecting exactly the kind of leadership image you want to project, and you are being recognized for it. Whatever you're doing is working successfully in your favor. As nobody is perfect, there are always pieces that don't fall into this spot at the moment, but as this section expands, your reputation will shift from being someone who *can* embody those strengths at times, to someone who consistently and reliably *does*.

## 3. *Reverse-Engineering Your Communication Style*

With that in mind, in the rest of this book, we will "reverse engineer" your communication style to determine what you are doing in your communication that is *causing* this gap, and figure out how to close it once and for all.

As a linguist, I'll show you the inner workings of why you are—or are not—influential and effective as a speaker. We'll identify the gap between what you think and want to convey, and how it actually "lands" in the other person's mind, and why. Then we'll explore some common communication pitfalls that can sabotage your success, and discuss better alternatives to maximize your powers of influence.

Most importantly, I promise you that we will do it all in a way that honors who you are, your values and beliefs, and your natural personality. I'm not trying to turn you into a "mini-me," "Stepford Wife," or corporate automaton. You will learn perspectives and skills that you can use (or not use) as you like and when you choose because you believe they will further your goals—and you will do so in a way that is 100% authentically *you*.

## IV.  LOOKING AHEAD

In the next chapter we'll drill down into both what creates the image of leadership and what creates your blind spot. We'll outline a simple framework for how to recognize the factors that determine whether or not we are able to project credibility and feel authentic at the same time. (Hint: It's virtually impossible to have one without the other.)

Then Chapters 3, 4, and 5 will each address in depth one of the three broad categories of communication cues identified in Chapter 2. You will learn to see and hear yourself through a new lens, and discover your hidden blind spots.

Chapter 6 answers a nagging question: "Can I change the way I communicate, using all the strategies discussed in Chapters 3, 4, and 5, and still be myself?" Discovering the key to doing so is essential to unlocking the growth potential within you.

Chapter 7 pivots from individual behaviors to how they affect your results in different contexts, ranging from conference calls to networking meetings to formal presentations and beyond.

Chapter 8 looks at the other half of the communication conversation: Listening. If your instinctive response to this is a reluctant, "Yeah, I know, my (spouse/boss/friends/kids/other) always complain that I don't listen to them," then this chapter is for you. Then again, if you're frustrated that people don't listen to *you,* particularly in more heated conversations, this chapter is for you too....

Finally, Chapter 9 helps you get a clearer vision of what is possible. It looks at some of the challenges of putting these guidelines into practice and offers some strategic and practical tips for doing so in a way that will help you get unstuck quickly and to easily reach your goals.

## V. POINTS OF IMPACT

1. Leadership is an image you create, regardless of your role or position.
2. Influence includes but is not limited to persuasion, and its effects are visible even when you are not present.
3. Your communication style will create an organizational culture by identifying and modeling what matters most to you. That will be the foundation of your legacy.
4. To achieve your desired degree of influence, you have to be willing and able to identify your blind spot and close the gap between how you want others to perceive you, how you think others perceive you, and how others actually perceive you.

## VI. BLIND-SPOT CHALLENGE: CREATE A BASELINE

Video record yourself as if you were talking to someone about an important topic, with the goal of getting them to respond in a certain way—however you want to define that.

- Speak for one or two minutes. Possible topics might include pitching or suggesting a product, service, or idea to a client, boss, employee, the board, a family member, neighbor, or your child's principal.
- Do NOT overprepare. Take a moment to organize your thoughts, then just *be yourself*. This is not a Hollywood production, so you should *not* rehearse or re-record until perfect. The goal is simply to get a clear picture of your usual, *unrehearsed* communication style.
- Stand up and set the camera (such as on your smartphone or laptop) so that it records your full body, head to toe, while you speak.
- DO NOT WATCH YOUR VIDEO...yet.

# CHAPTER 2

## WHAT MAKES SPEECH INFLUENTIAL?

---

*'In that case,' said the Dodo solemnly, rising to its feet, 'I move that the meeting adjourn, for the immediate adoption of more energetic remedies—'*

*'Speak English!' said the Eaglet. 'I don't know the meaning of half those long words, and, what's more, I don't believe you do either!' And the Eaglet bent down its head to hide a smile: some of the other birds tittered audibly.*

—Lewis Carroll. *Alice's Adventures in Wonderland.*

---

## I.   WHY DO PEOPLE "GET ON BOARD" WITH ANYTHING?

When I talk about getting people "on board," I'm not talking about people who, at best, have verbally said "yes" and are mechanically going through the motions because they're supposed to, or, at worst, because they recognize the threat of some negative consequence if they don't. That's merely *enlisting* them, at which point their investment in the issue at hand is only an inch deep.

Don't enlist people, *enroll* them. Enrolling people in your vision and getting them on board with it requires helping them to recognize the inherent value in it. Moreover, they need to see their own participation in achieving that vision as a matter of personal importance, even if the original vision wasn't their idea in the first place. You want to know that they are all-in, heart, mind, body, and soul.

What gets people on board like that? Simply put, you have to make them not only think, you have to make them *feel*. When their thoughts and feelings are aligned with yours, it will compel them to take action, which is where the rubber meets the road. When this starts to become a pattern, it becomes a reflection of your brand.

Marketers live by the rule of thumb that customers have to *know, like,* and *trust* a brand, in order to maintain and increase that brand's customer base. For some people, that might mean knowing that a cosmetics company does not engage in animal testing of their products, that a car model leaves a significantly smaller carbon footprint or will last 300,000 miles, or that the coffee bean farmers and roasters in developing countries were paid fair wages. Marketers know that the emotional and psychological benefits people get from these products and services will often be what persuades people to buy them—even when a similar but significantly cheaper alternative is available.

Similarly, when people start to know, like, and trust *your* brand, they will be more willing to give you the benefit of the doubt, to help you turn your vision into reality. They recognize that even though there may be a temporary cost (like longer hours to meet a deadline or a steep learning curve when a new system is implemented), the end result has an inherent value—a value that speaks to them both logically and emotionally—and a benefit that outweighs the cost. At that point, they trust that you will deliver what you promise.

## II.  THE ROLE OF AUTHENTICITY AND PERSUASION

The way you communicate your vision plays a critical role in its logical and emotional appeal and is a preeminent factor in whether or not you will successfully enroll people in it. Each subsequent conversation you have about it will either reinforce your brand's promise or undermine it. In order for a vision to be persuasive and compelling, the vision itself and the way you share it must come across as sincere and authentic.

## III.  DEFINING YOUR VISION

What *is* your vision? Do you even have one? As the Cheshire Cat may have asked, "Where do you want to go?" Simply put, your vision is about the future *impact* you want to have. You will have goals along the way, measurable milestones that indicate whether or not you are making progress, but a vision is not something that is ever measurably finished and complete.

For example, having the largest market share in your industry or getting a $1 billion IPO valuation is a great long-term goal to strive for, but it's not a vision. Why? Because it doesn't express *why* you want to achieve it, or what impact it will have if you are successful. So, why does it matter? Why should anyone care?

When Dr. Martin Luther King gave his famous "I have a dream" speech, his speech was not about passing legislation to give African Americans equal rights. Of course, that was the *goal* of the speech, the measurable result of its success. But the vision—the dream, as it were—was that "...little black boys and black girls will be able to join hands with little white boys and white girls as sisters and brothers." That societal transformation would be the impact of such legislation, and the vision tugged at people's heartstrings, making them willing to risk their own safety and the safety of their families in order to achieve it.

Think about it: In sharing his vision, wouldn't Dr. King's message have landed differently if, instead of "I have a dream," his refrain had been, "I have a goal?"

At the foundation of influence is being clear on what your own vision is. Whether it's for your company, your career, or even your family, do you have a vision in mind? What legacy do you want to leave? Can you articulate it clearly and concisely so that others understand it? And if so, will they think it is worth getting on board?

Once you have your vision, the challenge becomes how to get there.

## IV.  GOAL-SETTING TO ACHIEVE YOUR VISION

Yogi Berra was famous for two things: being an iconic baseball player, manager, and ultimately coach of the New York Yankees...and speaking in fractured metaphors and using close-but-no-cigar expressions, like "When you come to a fork in the road, take it." For our purposes here, my favorite Yogi Berra quote is, "If you don't know where you're going, you might end up someplace else."

When it comes to establishing your leadership image and reputation, and laying the groundwork for your vision and legacy, every interaction you have will take you either another step toward achieving your vision, or a step away from it. You *do* have control over which direction you move. The question becomes: do you *choose* the direction of your path and destination, or do you let chance decide for you? The answer will be determined in great part by whether or not you set the right goals along the way, large and small, and goal-setting requires strategic *planning.*

*Janet came to me as a result of having been passed over for an executive promotion in favor of someone else whom she believed was less qualified. By working with me, she hoped to close the gap on some of the leadership communication skills her boss had previously indicated would be necessary to be ready for such a promotion.*

*By the end of our initial consultation, Janet had become clear on her two-fold goal for the conversation she needed to have with her boss: She needed answers regarding what was needed for a promotion, and she needed budget approval for coaching. Her challenge was how to get everything she wanted out of that conversation without letting her emotions take over, coming across as angry or frustrated, or putting her boss on the defensive.*

*In the end, I suggested: "Why not approach him and tell him you're glad to have this opportunity to talk to him, because the timing is great. Explain that in light of [your colleague's] promotion, you are all the more committed to working on yourself and your leadership. Then you can mention that since he had previously indicated explicitly that you needed to work on your communication skills, you took initiative and found a coach you think would be ideal. Then, after discussing whatever other details you need to cover about coaching, you could end the meeting* with, 'By the way, I was curious about one more thing. What was it that [name of colleague] did to help you see her as being ready for the role? Because I know she had stuff to work on as well.'"

At that point Janet sat upright with a big smile and said, "That's awesome! That's perfect. That way I can show that I'm actually taking his feedback seriously, so it sounds like this is his idea I'm executing. I still get the answers I want, but I'm not coming across as being jealous or angry, and it puts everything into perspective. It's all just so positive. What's there to say no to?"

Fortunately, her boss couldn't find anything to say no to either, and we started working together a few weeks later. It was all because she got clear on her goals and walked into that meeting with a plan.

To begin with, you need to ask yourself key questions, such as:

- What is my desired outcome for this exchange or event?
- Do I want them to ask me more questions?
- Do I want them to give me a promotion, or to buy my product or service?
- Do I want them to simply acknowledge the validity of a point I made, even if they don't change their minds?

Whether you're heading into a one-on-one interaction, participating in or facilitating a meeting, or giving a formal presentation, you need a goal...and a plan. Once that is set, then you have to shift your focus from the message to the messenger.

## V. BET THE JOCKEY, NOT THE HORSE

In order to achieve your goal, ask yourself what kind of messenger would be most successful in getting through to your audience. In other words, what qualities do you need your audience to see in you? Do you want them to see you as competent, confident, or authoritative? Do you want them to see you as sympathetic, approachable, or trustworthy? Maybe you need to be seen as friendly, disarming, charming, and engaging, or even fun, energetic, and enthusiastic. There is no wrong answer. It is a matter of choice, so really think about how you want those particular people to perceive you, and what qualities you want them to recognize in you.

I'm not suggesting you pretend to be someone you're not—on the contrary, you need to be completely *authentic* in your delivery, just letting your version of those qualities shine through. In the end, you do have the ability to control the way you come across to someone, and to influence the way you are perceived based upon the way you communicate. This is one of the most influential factors in determining whether or not you reach your intended goal.

Venture capitalists have an expression, "Bet the jockey, not the horse." This means that ultimately the horse is just the vehicle, but a skilled jockey can make a horse win, even if the horse isn't the favorite. On the other hand, a subpar jockey can take a horse that *should* win and end up coming in second or worse. It's logical enough, but how is this relevant to business investing?

Years ago, I was a partner in a tech startup that was invited to participate in DreamIt Ventures, a tech startup incubator program in Philadelphia. Among the various visitors and guest speakers who came to offer their advice and support were Marv Goldman and his team from Apex Ventures, a major venture capital investment company. They went around to each team to hear about their app designs, look at prototypes, and offer perspective and feedback. When they came to our table, I explained the need we were trying to fill, the benefits of our product, and how it would achieve the promised results. They asked questions and offered suggestions. When they were getting ready to move on to the next team, Marv shook my hand and said, "Good luck. I'm inspired."

Now, we had expected and hoped to hear general praise for a good idea and an interesting design, etc. but this particular praise caught me by surprise. At the end of the day, as the Apex Ventures team was preparing to leave, I stopped them at the door and asked Marv what about the app, specifically, he had found inspiring. He paused for a moment and then said, "It wasn't the app, it was you. I really felt your passion, I understood very clearly what you wanted to do and why, and I believed that you could do it."

The lesson to take from this is that *people will only buy into your vision, message, product, service, or "horse" if they first buy into YOU*. You are your brand. For people to be voluntarily willing to get on board with your vision and help you turn it into reality, your brand and your vision must be compelling and must be delivered in an equally compelling manner.

> **People will only buy into your vision,**
> **message, product, service, or "horse"**
> **if they first buy into YOU.**

So how can you do this? How can you be the right kind of jockey? What is that X-factor?

# VI. COMMUNICATION AND EXECUTIVE PRESENCE

## A. Executive Presence

Executive presence—sometimes referred to as *leadership presence* or *command presence*—is one of the hottest topics in research and discussions about leadership. It's also the most common reason people contact me for coaching. They realize they lack executive presence, but they don't know why, what they're doing wrong, or what to do about it. But they *do* realize that it's why they're not having their desired impact.

Part of the challenge is that executive presence is hard to define. It's not a single characteristic that you either have or you don't; it's the *effect* that is the *result* of a whole constellation of qualities and characteristics. Moreover, these characteristics are not universally defined; everyone seems to come up with their own list. While the labels, categories, and arrangements they use vary, they all include similar concepts. What strikes me as most interesting, however, is that while having good communication skills is universally recognized as being of critical importance, it is invariably listed as a separate quality or category. As I see it, however, communication skill directly influences virtually every other factor.

For example, one of the most commonly referenced desirable qualities is *gravitas*. Gravitas is not just about being serious or "grave." Of course, there's a time and place for that too, but gravitas is bigger than that. Among

23

other components, it encompasses the importance of having technical expertise, knowledge and experience, and confidence and resilience; being willing to take risks and stand up for what you believe in; being able to show grace under fire; and having the confidence to make decisions and see them through, even when they—and you—might be unpopular as a result.

But having those qualities isn't enough. Technical expertise will only get you so far, unless you learn how to convey that expertise in a way that is clear and compelling to others who are *not* similarly expert in your field. Additionally, your confidence can't just be internal; for others to see it, it has to come through in your voice and your body language. And executing those unpopular decisions needs to be done in a way that doesn't turn "grace under fire" into a trail of burned bridges.

Even your appearance is influenced by your communication. For example, when you're presenting to the board, if you are fidgeting, picking at your cuticles, playing with your mustache, or shifting uncomfortably from one foot to the other, nobody will notice if you're wearing an Armani power suit. Although your suit tries to say *I'm confident and powerful*, the truth is that inside, you're uncomfortable and insecure, and everyone knows it.

Upon watching a three-second snippet of someone who speaks shyly or awkwardly, you can identify a variety of factors that seem to contribute to that impression, but it's hard to isolate one or another as being "the most important." This is because it's not just the individual factors themselves, but how they interact with each other that has a direct influence on the impression you make. Rarely do these factors work in isolation and how they are combined directly dictates people's evaluation of your executive presence. So, what's the solution?

## B.  Vocal Executive Presence: Command the Room, Connect with the Audience, Close the Deal

Under the broad umbrella of executive presence, my work is in what I refer to as "vocal executive presence." This means both your literal voice and your figurative ("author's") voice. It's about what your ideas are, how you frame them, and how you deliver them in a way that lets you accomplish three ultimate goals...what I refer to as the "Three Cs" of vocal executive presence: Command the room, Connect with the audience, and Close the deal.

**Command the room,
Connect with the audience, and
Close the deal.**

## 1.   Command the Room

You don't have to be a towering six-foot-five and two hundred fifty pounds to *command the room*. I'm five-foot-one on a good day, and high heels don't add enough to make a noticeable difference, so relying on my size to command people's attention would be a lost cause. It has to be about more than that.

Commanding a room is about being able to get people's attention in the first place—and hold it. Without having to demand it explicitly, there something in your demeanor that says *I need to be listened to and you need to hear what I have to say,* or *I have something I need to tell you or ask, and you need to listen because it's important.* The other half of that equation is in getting your audience to agree, consciously or subconsciously, to turn their attention to you.

Everyone likes the idea of having a captive audience, but to me, a captive is a prisoner, so a captive audience is one that has no choice but to sit and listen, since they're not allowed to leave. This is the status of most professional audiences in meetings, conferences, workshops, and presentations, but is it how you *want* people to feel when you talk?

I think what's more important is to have a *captivated* audience. A captivated audience is mesmerized, engrossed in the presentation. They forget they're holding a cell phone with all sorts of temptations at their fingertips...they're not "multitasking," checking text messages, writing emails, or sending tweets. They are concentrating on you because of the way you hold yourself, the way you deliver your message, the quality of your content, the intrigue of your topic, and the way you make it meaningful for them. That's commanding the room.

## 2.   Connect with the Audience

Connecting with the audience is about relevance. It is so important, and this is where so many speakers and presenters, in formal and informal situations alike, lose their audience before they even start. Ideally, you need your audience to connect with two things: whatever you're talking about, and you.

Content-wise, if you have important information to share, it's critical that you frame it in a way that is directly relevant to your listeners, where they understand its importance for them individually and its value to the company or to society. They need to see themselves in whatever person or scenario you're discussing, in order to empathize with it. It's not just about sharing data, it's about *telling the story* of the data.

But sharing meaningful information isn't enough to establish a connection. The audience needs to recognize that *you* are connected mentally and emotionally to the topic. If you just go through your data or your agenda point by point, sounding like you're doing it because you have to, or like you'd rather be anywhere else but here, you're missing the boat.

Think about it: If it doesn't sound like you're interested in your own information, why would anyone else be? When you sound like you mean what you say, and you convey a sense of not just what people should think, but how they should *feel* about it and *why*, your audience is more likely to feel a connection to what you are saying—even if they don't necessarily *agree* with it. And, if you can make them feel connected to your message, they will feel connected with you as the messenger.

You'll recognize that you are connecting when your audience is looking at you and nodding, or they have their heads cocked to one side, deep in thought as they consider and weigh what you're saying. Even if they are challenging some of your points, they're *engaged*, captivated. That's connecting with the audience.

### 3.   Close the Deal

In the end, you need to *close the deal*. Closing the deal doesn't necessarily mean getting a signature on the check (although that's always a good thing). It's about getting to *yes*. And that *yes* could be coming to an agreement on a new project timeline, or an agreement to reconvene later to discuss additional details and next steps. Maybe it's getting someone to make an introduction, or reevaluate a budget. When you know the outcome you want to achieve, each *yes* means another step toward it. That's closing the deal.

When you have mastered the Three Cs, you've solidified your vocal executive presence. The beauty is that you don't have to be at the top of the ladder to master the art. Vocal executive presence can—and *should*—be something you aim to exude at any level, and in any situation.

This is what I want for you—in reading this book and in following my suggestions. I want you to be able to speak so naturally, so clearly and comfortably, so engagingly and appropriately in any context that people can't help but sit up, pay attention, and notice that there's something special about you. I want you to rise above the others and to be so good at speaking that people can't *not* notice. I want them to be drawn in.

So, what does it take to master the Three Cs?

## C.  Credibility

In establishing your vocal executive presence and successfully mastering the Three Cs, there is one core factor, one perception that is a prerequisite to all the rest. It's the notion of *credibility*.

Part of the challenge is that, whether speaking in meetings, webinars, presentations, or other contexts, it seems as though holding people "captive," rather than "captivated," has become the accepted norm. The only expected requirement is that a speaker's facts and data be correct. Often, a speaker's presence neither commands the room nor connects them with the audience, so they rely on their material to close the deal for itself. At best, the typical communication style these days is mediocre, but mediocrity is not influential, because mediocrity does not inspire *credibility*.

Okay, so what makes someone credible?

At one time or another, we've all had that conversation where one person gets upset and the other says, "What? Why are you mad? What did I say?" to which the response is, "It's not what you said, it's how you said it!" Actually, it's both. The problem is that regardless of what was said, there was something in the way it was presented that instilled in the listener an overwhelming sense of doubt. This disconnect between message content and delivery is what causes the vast majority of misunderstandings, and more importantly, creates confusion because the speaker is wholly unaware of any mismatch. The solution begins with an awareness of why and how it occurs.

In spoken communication, there is a core message. Whether you realize it or not, to be credible, you need to communicate that message through three different channels all at the same time. They are the Three Vs: Verbal, Vocal, and Visual.

## 1. Verbal

The first channel is the verbal channel. This is the "What you say" part of your message. It's the words you choose, the "text" of your message... what we would see in your transcript. This is where most people spend the majority of their time and effort, hoping their expertise is going to shine through in their content.

Unfortunately, being factually correct isn't enough. For example, the diplomacy, organization, and anecdotes of your argument all play a part in the impact your words have on your audience. And, needless to say, you will need to explain the same core message differently depending upon whether you're presenting to a group of experts or non-experts. For example, when you are preparing your content, start by asking yourself these questions:

- "Am I giving sufficient detail, excessive detail, or omitting key details?
- What about my vocabulary? Is it overly simple, or is it too technical? Am I using too much jargon?
- Am I explaining things clearly, so that others can understand what I'm saying? If they don't share my expertise, am I presenting the material in a way that doesn't seem like I'm talking down to them, or talking over their heads?"

All of these areas and more are fundamentally important, but your words in and of themselves don't convey your entire message. In particular, they fail to transmit the true feelings or intent behind what you are saying. That comes through in the next two channels.

## 2. Vocal

Next, there's the vocal channel. This taps into the first half of the "how you say it" challenge. Regardless of what you decide to say in your verbal content, the vocal channel considers the sound of those exact words as they're coming out of your mouth. It's amazing how we judge people based on this factor. We judge their mood. We judge their sincerity. We judge their maturity. We judge their competency, education, intelligence, and more.

In your vocal delivery, you have to factor in components like your volume, speed, pacing, tonality, breath support, and whether your voice sounds gravelly, breathy, or nasal.

Consider this: You walk into work with a new hairstyle. A colleague responds with two simple words: *Nice haircut.* Written down, these two words seem simple enough, but the way they *sound* will tell you what your colleague actually *means.* Are they being sincere and complimentary? Are they impressed? Are they being sarcastic because they think it looks awful? Or are they just mumbling a few perfunctory words of flattery because they think they have to acknowledge it out of social obligation, but otherwise couldn't care less? Without ever looking at their face, you have an instant, instinctual sense for whether you *want* to respond with, "Thanks!" or... something slightly less polite.

## 3.  *Visual*

The final channel is the visual channel. This is the other half of the "how you say it" piece. The visual channel is what many people refer to as "nonverbal" communication or "body language," otherwise known as paralinguistic cues, such as facial expressions, gestures, and posture (whether you are sitting or standing). It also includes things like how you're groomed or dressed, because that's the wrapping paper that the message comes in.

Imagine watching yourself on video with the sound off. What do you infer about the speaker (in this case, yourself) based solely on what you see? That's what you are communicating visually.

You can tell a lot about a person—at least about how they seem to feel in the moment, and even about their personality—based on physical cues: whether or not they smile in the middle of a conversation or keep a stone face the entire time, whether they pick at their fingernails, gesticulate wildly, or don't move at all. If, for example, you ask someone a question and they roll their eyes before they even begin to speak, you know you're not going to like the answer.

When you speak, your audience is always consciously or subconsciously evaluating your credibility based on what they infer from these three channels—the Three Vs: verbal, vocal, and visual. Remember we talked earlier about the concept of betting on the jockey rather than the horse? People have to buy into you before they'll buy your product, service, proposal, or idea, and the way you balance the Three Vs is what will convince them to place their bets on you.

## 4. *Alignment*

When all three of these channels are conveying the same message at the same time, you are in *alignment*. And within that alignment, the audience just has to pay attention to one single, unified, three-dimensional message. All signals are reinforcing each other in harmony, as the following diagram shows. Note how there is a "V" reinforcing each physical corner of the triangle.

**Figure 2: Message Alignment**

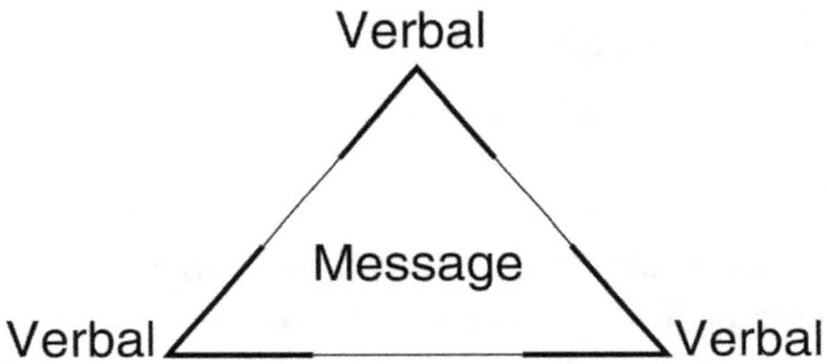

Verbal

Message

Verbal                    Verbal

As a result, that alignment creates a strong foundation of credibility, and credibility is the cornerstone of true leadership and influence.

**Alignment creates a strong foundation of credibility,
and credibility is the cornerstone
of true leadership and influence.**

A problem arises, however, if one or more of those channels is out of alignment: when the words, the voice, and the body language don't match. When they are out of alignment, the picture changes. The different channels send conflicting and even competing messages, so it is confusing to the audience. Inside the person's brain, what they're receiving is this:

**Figure 3: Speaking out of Alignment**

Verbal Message

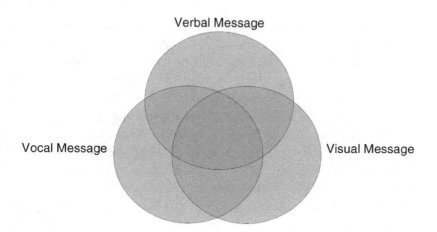

Vocal Message

Visual Message

You've got three different channels, each sending a different message. When that happens, even though *some* of the message components might align, as represented by the part of the diagram above where all three circles intersect, the audience can't focus on that part, because they are too distracted and confused by the mixed messages, as represented by the other sections of the diagram with only partial overlap, or none at all. And, truth be told, it's almost never just one detail that's out of sync with the rest. If you can identify one or two elements that are out of sync, there's usually a whole constellation of other mixed signals you're also sending off without even knowing it. When that happens, even if they think your product is good or that your idea is solid, doubt starts to creep in. You have undermined your own authority and credibility.

Imagine, for example, that you are interviewing for a job as a CEO. You may be arguing that you are the best person for this leadership opportunity, but if you are talking quickly, touching your face subconsciously, and peppering your answers with fillers like "Uh, uh, I mean, well, you know," although your resume may look great and all your claims regarding your accomplishments and goals may be true, the fact is, you don't come across as "CEO material." You don't have a CEO presence about you, so they're not buying it. The misalignment undermined your credibility.

## 5. Myth-busting

One of the most maddening myths I hear is when people say things like, "Well, you know fifty-five percent of all communication is nonverbal." Wrong.

What research[3] has shown is that comparatively, when you're *out of alignment*, the impression that sticks with the audience is disproportionately influenced by your visual communication—about fifty-five percent. What this indicates is that if the visual messaging doesn't match up with the other channels, people believe what they see more than what they hear.

Subsequently, about thirty-eight percent of an audience's impression of you and your credibility is based on the sound of your voice, specifically your tonality, meaning your pitch variation—again, when you are *out* of alignment. You've probably done the math already, but that leaves a paltry seven percent of the audience's subconscious evaluation of your credibility to be based on your words alone (*"what* you say") when they are *not* in alignment with your other communication channels (*"how* you say it.")

What this tells us is that even when an audience is paying attention, unless your verbal, vocal, and visual communication are working in harmony, how you deliver a message makes a much stronger gut-level impression than what you say. If you typically rely on just the inherent quality of your content to carry you through, hoping or assuming that because you're smart or an expert that your voice and your physical communication don't matter, think again.

You can't afford to gamble that your content is going to be so solid that even if your delivery is totally flat or off, it'll be "good enough." If you're going to rely on the content speaking for itself, then you probably should let it do so, and either email it to people so that all they see is the text and the graphics and can go through it at their own pace and convenience, or get somebody else to present it. It's not just a matter of your delivery adding extra quality to the message content; it's about ensuring that you're not actively detracting from its credibility—and yours.

This is not to say that your audience won't believe the math in your spreadsheets. The math is the math. The computer doesn't make

---

[3] Mehrabian, Albert, and Morton Wiener. "Decoding of Inconsistent Communications." *Journal of Personality and Social Psychology* 6.1 (1967): 109-114.

computational errors, but your *claims* about the spreadsheet are all open for interpretation. It's about enrolling people in your vision. It's about the data's implications and about what decisions should be made as a result of it. Especially if you're saying something that's controversial or risky that may not be met with enthusiasm, this is where the data cannot stand for itself. This is where the data relies on how you frame it in your delivery, your voice, and your body language, along with your word choice, to drive the point home. That's critical. That's where the power of your *influence* becomes visible.

## 6.  Alignment and Your Credibility

Where and how does this apply to us? Basically, everywhere and in all ways. The antidote to being out of alignment and losing credibility is to be *aware of* and *prepare for* your verbal content *and* your vocal and visual delivery, no matter what kind of interaction you're walking into.

Ask yourself: "How do I prepare to present to the board or the executive team? How do I prepare for an investor or for a conference presentation? For my annual review? For our weekly team meeting?" If you're like most people, you put about ninety-nine percent of your prep time into the content, into the reports, the spreadsheets, and the slides. You certainly don't put half of your prep time or more into the delivery. For that matter, you're probably not even putting a tenth of your preparation efforts into your delivery. Most people scramble up to the last minute just to get the content down on paper, then they wing the delivery. Maybe they "rehearse" in their head while walking or driving to the meeting, but that's about it.

If that's the case with you, then ask yourself: "When I'm winging the delivery, no matter how formal or informal the situation, what are the odds that I am completely in alignment?" If you're being honest, you'll probably admit it's not very high. You may stumble over your words a bit, trying to figure out what you want to say next. Your voice may end up sounding a little flat or nervous. If you're sitting with your hands in your lap, you might fidget, or if you're standing, you might be shifting your weight from foot to foot—all without realizing it.

But one way or another, you're not projecting the image of someone who believes 100 percent in what they're saying. It's not inherently obvious that you're 100 percent clear on your vision, 100 percent clear on your message, 100 percent clear in your reasoning, or 100 percent confident that they will—or even should—see your vision and get on board with it.

If you can't convince your audience in your delivery that you are 100 percent clear on these things, they will not be 100 percent clear on them either. If anything, the lack of clarity is dissuasive. Without this certainty, you are not credible. Without credibility, there is no influence. Nobody is going to bet on that jockey.

In Part 2 of this book, we're going to break down each of these Three V channels to look more carefully at the verbal, the vocal, and the visual messaging cues, so you can understand their impact, how they work, what their components are, and how you can learn to master all of them in building your vocal executive presence. Then you can ensure that no matter what situation you walk into, you've mastered the Three Cs, so you can always command the room, connect with the audience, and close the deal.

## VII. POINTS OF IMPACT

1. Rather than enlisting people in your plan, you need to enroll them in your vision so they see their role in it and its benefits and value for them. Projecting sincerity and authenticity is necessary to achieve this result.
2. Vision is big-picture: It gives you something worth working towards, so you are always striving to improve and expand your desired impact.
3. Set goals with an explicit plan for execution to reach the vision.
4. People must buy into you before they buy into your product, service, or idea.
5. Executive presence is necessary if you want others to see you as a leader. Communication should not be viewed as a separate and decontextualized skill area of its own in the context of executive presence because it affects all other areas.
6. Mastering executive presence requires mastery of the Three Cs of vocal executive presence. It all helps to capture and hold the audience's attention...and get to yes!

7. Alignment of the Three Vs: verbal, vocal, and visual channels, leads to credibility, which is at the foundation of your leadership image.

# VIII. BLIND SPOT CHALLENGE: FIRST IMPRESSIONS

Now watch your baseline video—just once, imagining that you are your intended audience.

- Ask yourself: "On an instinctive, gut-level, what impression does the person in that video make?" Write it down, describing it in as much detail as you can. You don't need to be "scientific" in your answers. For example, it's fine to write, "I don't know why but there was something annoying in the way he sounded," or "She sounded condescending," or, "I really liked the guy—he seemed like someone I'd want to grab a beer with, but I'm not sure if he struck me as executive material."
- Now ask yourself: "If the person in that video was talking to me, what would be my response to them, and why?" Write this down too, being objective, honest, and specific in your answer.

# CHAPTER 3

## VERBAL

---

*... 'There's glory for you!'*

*'I don't know what you mean by "glory,"' Alice said.*

*Humpty Dumpty smiled contemptuously. 'Of course you don't— till I tell you. I meant 'there's a nice knock-down argument for you!''*

*'But 'glory' doesn't mean 'a nice knock-down argument,'' Alice objected.*

*'When I use a word,' Humpty Dumpty said in rather a scornful tone, 'it means just what I choose it to mean—neither more nor less.'*

*'The question is,' said Alice, 'whether you can make words mean so many different things.'*

*'The question is,' said Humpty Dumpty, 'which is to be master— that's all.'*

—Lewis Carroll. *Through the Looking-Glass.*

---

## I.  WHY DO WORDS MATTER?

This seems like a silly question in some ways. Words are the essence of your message. If you are writing to someone, whether in an email, a text message, or an old-fashioned letter or birthday card, your words are all they have to go on—short of drawings or increasingly popular "emojis"—to understand the meaning and purpose of what you want to tell them.

If your goal is to maximize your ability to influence others' thinking and behavior, at its core, the root content of your message needs to be crystal clear. The words you choose, your accuracy and jargon, your degree of detail and diplomacy, and the organization of your thoughts are all at the root. When the root content is well developed, the foundation of your message is strong.

When you are working with the First C—*command the room*—you need to make sure that your verbal content is logical and speaks to the needs, interests, and emotional temperament of your target audience. Are your words accurate, relevant, and essential, or are they vague, tangential, or excessively detailed? Do they elevate, educate, and empower? What about the degree of technicality in your material? Does your audience have to be an expert to follow your jargon, or do you explain it in a way that any interested person can understand? Not to mention, there's always the internal tug-of-war between diplomacy and directness: at what point does "diplomatic" slide into excessive sugar-coating and avoiding the real issue? On the other hand, where is the line between being "direct" and "blunt," even hurtful? Your voice, body language, and facial expressions can be perfect, but if your words are off, the foundation of your message is weak and will not lead to your desired result.

At the very least, your words have to be accurate. When I was a child, my father would sometimes make a slip of the tongue such as saying "... when you go to school tomorrow," on a Friday. Since "tomorrow" was a Saturday, we would leap at his error and exclaim, "Tomorrow?!" Dad was ready with a favorite response: "Listen to what I mean, not what I say."

Now that example is innocuous enough, but many people seem to operate under the misimpression that as long as their words get the main idea across, it's good enough. It's not.

In speech, your word choice can convey countless underlying details, such as telling someone, directly or indirectly, that you are trying to include them or exclude them from participating in a conversation. For example, if you are with two people who are discussing a meeting they attended together in which you did not take part, they have three choices.

- First, they can continue to rehash details between them and ignore you and the fact that you can't participate since you don't have the background. This option is *exclusive* in nature, whether they are doing it intentionally (which is passive-aggressive and socially rude), or unintentionally (in which case they are oblivious to the fact that you are left out).

■ Second, they can provide you with additional information so you are up to speed and can participate more fully in the conversation. This is *inclusive* and *collaborative*. Your two colleagues are ensuring that you are *not* left out.

■ Third, they can change the topic to something more relevant to all three of you. Maybe the original issue wasn't particularly time-sensitive and there was no need to include you in that discussion. Such a change in subject would be an effort both to include you in the conversation of the moment and to exclude you from the details of the aforementioned meeting. In this case, you could interpret their intentions in a variety of ways, depending on whether or not you *wanted* to be in on that meeting in the first place.

Your words also show your level of expertise and understanding. Of course, part of the way people want you to demonstrate your expertise is to explain things to them in a way that they can understand easily and simultaneously makes them *feel* smart, even though they are *not* experts. That's why avoiding unnecessary jargon and overly technical details is critical. Unfortunately, when presenters feel insecure, their instinct is to do just the opposite: They rely on lots of big words and technical details as a crutch to prove how smart they are, as if that will somehow compensate for the fact that they are not totally sure of what they are saying or that they are feeling self-conscious.

If you are familiar with any TED talks from some of the modern leadership gurus, such as Simon Sinek or Amy Cuddy, you know that the beauty of their performance is that they are using simple conversational language, yet they do not sacrifice meaning or credibility. In spite of their conversational style, you are still confident in their expertise.

Of course, if they were presenting their work at an academic conference, sharing some of the research on which they built their careers—and their TED talks—with other professors and researchers in similar fields, I am fairly certain their speech would be different. They would use lots of technical jargon and terms from psychology, game theory, and organizational dynamics and behavior, but that's because they'd be speaking to an audience who shares that language (or that *lexicon*, if I were writing this as an academic textbook).

Remember the second C? *Connect with the audience.* A critical rule of thumb is that you have to know your audience to determine what words will work best for the job. There is a big difference between the personal stories a presenter will tell when working with a room of venture capitalists and investors in Silicon Valley, for example, compared to when they are running a workshop for high school students. There is a relatability factor that begins with "speaking their language" fluently, even when the goal is to teach the audience the language of the presenter.

Here are some factors to consider when choosing your words in order to master all Three Cs.

## II.   FILLERS

I remember my third-grade teacher who, upon hearing anyone say "like" as anything other than a verb or simile, would quickly blurt out, "Like-like-like-like-like!" It worked well to condition a bunch of eight-year-olds to break a bad habit. Similarly, anyone who has ever attended a Toastmasters meeting has met the "um-counter," whose sole job it is to count the number of fillers you use during your speech, so you can attempt to do better next time, ideally with no fillers at all.

Fillers are those little words, non-words, and phrases such as *um, uh, like, I mean,* and *you know,* that get peppered throughout your speech. They're called "fillers" because they fill the silence that would otherwise be left as you hesitate to choose your next word, or decide what you want to say. Fillers leave the impression of uncertainty. While one or two may go unnoticed, too many will interrupt your flow of thought, chop up your sentence, make you sound tentative and doubtful, and ultimately undermine your authority.

An HR director once hired me specifically to help Jack, one of their senior executives, stop saying "you know." The problem was not the existence of the occasional filler, or even the annoyance of a frequently used one. The problem was that Jack used it *so* frequently that sometimes his coworkers would stop paying attention to what he was saying in meetings, and instead make tally marks on paper to count the number of times they heard it. Then they would compare "scores" with each other afterward! The HR director told me that one tally came to *nearly fifty instances in less than a four-minute stretch*. That's nearly one "you know" every 4.8 seconds!

More importantly, however, the effect of this bad habit was that the executive team had started denying Jack opportunities to speak at conferences and other events where his qualifications would have made him the natural choice. Remember: leadership is an image, and they felt that he would not reflect the right image for the organization until he got his "you know's" under control. In short, lacking that aspect of executive presence was completely undermining his credibility and influence.

There are also what I call "educated fillers," meaning words and phrases such as *actually, really,* and *basically,* which tend to fly under the radar because they are real words that sound "intelligent," but ultimately are sprinkled uselessly throughout people's speech the same way people use *like* or *um*.

At home a couple of years ago, I realized that my then-thirteen-year-old son had developed a habit of using "pretty much" as his filler of choice. One day mid-conversation I interrupted and said to him, "I challenge you to get through the rest of the story without saying 'pretty much.'" He shrugged as if to imply the quintessential teenage "whatever." He continued his story, and a moment later it slipped out again. I simply echoed: "Pretty much?" He rolled his eyes and repeated the sentence without the filler, but from then on, every time he said it, he caught himself and growled in frustration. The frustration was not so much that he used a filler, but that he had to admit that I was "right," which, of course, is the last thing most teenagers want to have to admit to a parent in such circumstances. Within a day or two, he had quickly broken himself of the "pretty much" habit.

Interestingly enough, *sometimes* inserting an occasional filler can be beneficial. I'm not suggesting you imitate a stereotypical "Valley-girl," littering your speech with *like* and other fillers. But if you find yourself in a position where your role or status might be intimidating, the (very) occasional *um*, or *you know* can make a conversation feel more casual, and put people at ease. This is also an important aspect of getting people to open their minds to your ideas: establishing comfort, which brings its own kind of influence.

# III. DIPLOMACY

The big question is when speech should, and should *not*, be personal. Naturally, you *DO* want to help people see how participation in your vision will benefit them personally; but you *DON'T* want to make personal insults if they disagree with you somehow. To ensure that you are appropriately balancing directness and diplomacy in each situation, there are two important rules of thumb.

## A. Objective vs. Subjective Language

The first rule to keeping your language diplomatic is knowing when and how to incorporate objective vs. subjective speech. *Objective* language is strictly fact-based, emotionally neutral, and opinion-free. *Subjective* language reflects opinions and can be emotionally charged. There is a time and a place for each. If you know that diplomacy will be paramount to a successful negotiation, such as when you are looking to discuss accountability or other sensitive issues where emotions could flare up and you want to avoid drama, make sure that your language stays objective and neutral.

For example, there is a big difference between hearing someone say, "There are some errors in your report that need to be addressed," and, "This report is garbage. You're useless—How can you be so incompetent?" Think about it: How would you feel if someone said each of those comments to you?

The first example is neutral, objective, incorporates passive voice ("...that need to be addressed,") and focuses on the report. It indirectly implies *who* needs to address them, but doesn't directly state or command it. As the writer of the report, hearing this news in this manner would allow you to find out what happened, clarify misunderstandings, apologize if needed, and fix the problem (and perhaps your reputation).

In contrast, the second approach is subjective and personal, focusing on you, the person who wrote the report, rather than on the report itself. It directly attacks your worth. It magnifies the initial embarrassment of having mistakes in your report, but beyond that, it evaluates your abilities overall, and identifies a reputation you would need to overcome to redeem yourself publicly. This kind of accusation makes your fight-or-flight reflexes kick in, which is unlikely to result in collaborative, efficient, or effective solutions, both short- and long-term.

Suzanne, a director at a marketing agency, was notorious for such blunt comments. She claimed that to do anything other than speak her mind directly was to be disingenuous and made her feel like she was "walking on eggshells." Needless to say, her comments were demoralizing to the staff and created unhealthy tension in the office.

She was frustrated that she often had to go back and have follow-up conversations with employees who did not make corrections to her standards the first time, and she became exasperated when an employee cried during one of her reprimands. "I've got a ton on my plate, and I don't have time to be all 'nicey-nicey' with everyone," she complained. "If they screwed up, they just need to own their mistake, suck it up and fix it."

I said, "There's an expression: If you don't have time to do something right, when will you have time to do it over? Have you heard that one?"

She slumped a bit in her chair. "No," she said with resignation, "but I get it."

"It's not about having time to be nicey-nicey. When you start the conversation with an attack on their personal value, their energy is so wrapped up in feelings of embarrassment, defensiveness, fear, anger, and more, they can barely focus on the nature of the problem you're actually trying to address. *They can't hear—much less process—what you're trying to say.* Not to mention they're no longer motivated by wanting to be a valuable contributor to the team. Those negative emotions take over, and that never results in optimal performance, which is why you often have to go back and speak to them a second or even a third time about the same problem that had only partially been fixed."

She agreed to work on focusing on the problem or disagreeing objectively with the content of someone's message rather than verbally attacking the person. This included phrasing her requests more conversationally, removing any unnecessary negative opinion language, such as *stupid,* and avoiding passive-aggressive rhetorical questions like, "What, are you trying to get me fired with this?"

The next week she came back with an incredulous smile. "I can't believe it," she said. "There's a guy at the office I've been butting heads with for over a year, and this week we actually sat down and had a really peaceful and productive meeting. It was hard to keep myself in check the whole time, but I did it, and it's amazing the difference it made!"

This practice of keeping language neutral and objective during difficult or awkward exchanges is just as effective outside of the office as it is in the workplace.

> *My friend Caroline called me recently, frustrated that her teenage son was becoming demanding, grumbling orders like, "Pick me up at 7:00" or "You need to drive my friends home." Her reflex was to yell at him for his "attitude," which would immediately escalate into a shouting match between them. I advised her to keep the discussion message-based rather than taking the emotional "bait" and launching into a lecture about his personal lack of gratitude and respect. After all, she still had the power to say no to his request.*
>
> *I said, "Try this: When he makes those demands, just stop and say, 'It sounded like there was a polite request for something in there, but I couldn't find it.' It focuses on the message, rather than the messenger, staying away from accusations or character judgments that could make him react defensively, and it implies that you're willing to say 'yes,' but only if he asks respectfully."*
>
> *She called me back a few days later, very happy to say that she had tried it out, and although he initially rolled his eyes at the comment, he did acquiesce with, "Mom, could you please pick me up at seven?" The next day when it happened again, she shortened her response to, "Was there a polite request in there somewhere?" and by the third day further truncated her reply to a single word: "Rephrase," which she found worked just as efficiently and effectively for text message exchanges as well.*
>
> *In the end, it was a win-win: her son got the support he wanted, and she got the respect she needed, and their relationship stayed healthy and open.*

Keeping negative, corrective feedback objective and non-personal allows people to hear and accept both what you say *and* what you mean.

## B.  Avoiding Absolutes

The other rule of thumb in maintaining a more diplomatic approach without sacrificing clarity is to avoid speaking in terms of absolutes. Absolutes are words that reflect a black-and-white, all-or-none assessment of the situation, such as:

- *all, always, every, everyone, everything, everywhere*
- *none, no, never, nobody, no one, nothing,* and *nowhere.*

If you tend to use these words during disagreements, you may *feel* like they add weight to your argument, but in reality they will weaken it. Unless your claim is indeed true 100% of the time, they overgeneralize the facts, and serve as exaggerations, which undermine credibility.

If you have lobbed unsubstantiated complaints along the lines of, "Nobody wants to work with him," or "I always have to do everything," the listener knows that emotions are running the show, and immediately starts to question the validity of your claim. Those claims harken back to childhood rants of, "You never let me do anything!" and "You always take his side!" Needless to say, the impression they make is not one of inspirational leadership.

More importantly, absolute terms like these bring discussions to a screeching halt. Maggie, for example, described herself as a very black-and-white thinker, and was known for digging her heels in during problem-solving meetings with comments like, "I'll never agree to that," or "There's no way that will work." The implication was, "I'm right, you're wrong, and until you accept that basic fact there's no point in continuing this conversation."

Instead, we explored more collaborative approaches to expressing disagreement, such as,

- "I'm having a really hard time seeing how..."
- "Help me understand why...," or
- "If that's the case, then what would happen to...?"

All of these keep the lines of communication open, and show that you want to work with the other person, not just force them to accept your side (no matter how certain you are that your perspective is correct.) At that point, at least one of two things is going to happen: either they are going to provide information that *does* clarify their point and helps you understand what they mean, *or* they are going to reveal where there is a hole in their theory. If it's the former, be ready to graciously acknowledge the newfound clarity and thank them for filling in the necessary blanks. If the latter, *also* be ready to graciously—not haughtily—point out the problem and how it supports your argument.

To this latter point, inside, you might *want* to say, "Ha! See? I told you so!" However, if you are trying to maintain a productive relationship with the other person, this is unadvisable. Instead, try something more charitable and instructive, such as, "Ah, now I see what the problem was...." The ability to maintain this kind of diplomatic touch is invaluable in establishing a shared sense of trust, which is a universally-accepted requirement in building your executive presence.

## IV. FEATURES VS. BENEFITS: WIIFM

In the art of persuasion, there's one factor that drives most human behavior: we are all self-centered, and directly or indirectly, we want the answer to one fundamental question for most decision-making. That simple five-word question is: "What's in it for me?" or WIIFM?

We are always looking for ways to persuade people, whether it's asking someone on the team to put in a few extra late nights to finish a project or asking your teenager to sacrifice time with his friends one evening to take care of a younger sibling when you have to be away at a business event. Often, they will do it (begrudgingly perhaps), but they will more willingly make a sacrifice if you frame your request in terms of how it will benefit them. It could be a financial reward, public recognition, enhanced social status, or just knowing that they will have your personal gratitude and respect as a result of their efforts and cooperation.

To ensure the WIIFM factor is addressed effectively, there's an important line to draw that many people don't recognize. That's the line between *features* and *benefits*.

Entrepreneurs and executives who need to pitch their product or service, particularly to investors, know this better than anyone. When entrepreneurs pitch effectively, they don't launch right into how many buttons and functions an app has, how the operating system works, or why the user interface is friendlier. Those are important features, but most people won't connect to them emotionally. Instead, their pitch starts right off the bat with the value the product brings to the user ultimately (i.e., its benefits).

That catches people's attention. People need to understand the "why" first, as Simon Sinek explains so well in his book, *Start With Why*. Once people understand why a product, service, or idea is of personal value, they're suddenly willing to listen to the other details, specifically *how* they can achieve that result. That's where the features come in.

On a broad level, think about any automobile commercial you've seen lately. Lincoln had an advertising campaign series featuring the actor Matthew McConaughey wearing an expensive suit, driving along Mulholland Drive or an equally iconic mountain road overlooking the romantic vista of the lights of Los Angeles at night. He doesn't talk about the amount of horse power in the car, the reliability of the mechanics, electricals, or the mileage. Nobody remembers what Matthew McConaughey said because Lincoln doesn't *want* you to focus on what he's talking about. For the most part he's rambling about nothing. His words are background noise, with the mellow ease of his voice setting a tone for the viewer's experience. Lincoln just wants you to focus on how you *feel* at that moment. They are advertising luxury, feeling relaxed, feeling sexy, powerful, and in control...and who doesn't want that? The idea is that if you can associate those benefits with that car, then that's incentive for you to buy the car. Advertisers know this.

But benefits need not be so superficial. For example, I worked with a sales director for a medical device company who was trying to help train hospital directors and physicians on how to explain a new product option to stroke patients. This little device was inserted by trans-catheter through a blood vessel in the groin into the heart, and closed off a section where clots could form, since there is a risk of clots going to the brain and causing a hemorrhage. It was a new alternative to taking the blood-thinner Warfarin as the typical means of preventing this risk after having a stroke.

The problem was that that's where the story was ending. The product wasn't compelling enough for patients. People would think, "Okay, I wouldn't have to take that medicine every day, but I'd have to have heart surgery. That doesn't sound like a better option!"

We realized that the description of taking medicine versus inserting a device was feature-focused, and lacked emotional appeal. So, I asked, "Why would people want this? What would be the benefit of surgery over taking medicine?"

The sales director explained. "Well, first," she said, "if you take Warfarin, there is always a risk of side effects, how it could interact with your other medications, and problems if you forget to take it or refill the prescription. None of that matters if you have (our device.)" She continued, "But more importantly, on Warfarin you have to go to a clinic at least once a month so they can test your blood to check your INR [internationally normalized ratio] to make sure you won't bleed out. But if you have (our device), you don't have to do that anymore. Once you've had your preliminary checkup or two with your doctor, you don't need regular monitoring; you're good to go."

"Let me get this straight," I said. "You're saying that if I don't need the medication, I don't need a monthly doctor's visit? That visit might take just thirty minutes, but when I factor in time sitting in the waiting room, plus the round-trip commute to a clinic that could be several hours away from my home, it could eat up the better part of a day. And if I'm unable to drive myself for whatever reason, it would save all that time for the person who gets stuck driving me too?"

"Yes," she said.

"Wow," I said. "At that point, what's at stake is quality of life! Imagine someone said to you they were going to give you an extra day of free time every month. Would that be valuable to you? To get back a day of paid or unpaid time off every month? Especially considering the fact that stroke survivors could live for another ten, twenty years or more, and many do go back to work upon recovery...that could add up to a lot of time lost in routine clinic visits, couldn't it!"

"I never thought about it that way," she said.

"But *that* is the real benefit to the patient. There's an emotional connection you can make with that benefit. That's what's in it for them."

Now, this example pertained to a specific product, but it's just as relevant when pitching an idea to a partner or presenting your vision to the board. Maybe you're pitching your own promotion and advocating for why you should be in line for the next CEO or CFO position. In these situations, what would you focus on instinctively? If you're like most people, you'd probably dive right into listing your qualifications, what you have accomplished, how long you've been there, how many roles you've taken, how well you know the customers, or how well you know the system.

Usually, you'll have to dig down two or three levels of asking yourself, "So what?" to identify and be able to articulate what a truly motivating factor would be for the listener. That's what you need to do to help them find a personal interest in getting on board and saying "yes," i.e., *Closing the deal.*

How much more persuasive would it be if you could flip each of those personal strength features around and explain why each has a specific, tangible benefit to the company? Sure, increasing revenue and saving money helps. But beyond that, the feature of having a more thorough knowledge of the technological infrastructure *and* a finance background, for example, may empower you with the skills to "translate" between the IT, finance, and business development departments, for example. Effective cross-functional communication can save a lot of time and prevent misunderstandings, which makes everybody's life less stressful and avoids costly errors in terms of time, money, manpower, and other resources.

Should a listener be able to deduce those implications from your list of skills and experience on your resume? Perhaps, but it may not happen right away. Plus, it's *so* much more compelling if you can clearly and simply articulate the relationship between them. That takes the burden of processing off the listener, and demonstrates the "strong communication skills" that your resume claims you have!

## V. MANAGING UP

Managing up is one of the hardest skill sets for many people to master, and it's one of the most crucial in projecting leadership, because of the specific relationship involved. "Managing up" refers to everything from synthesizing data for higher-ups and boards of directors, to pitching ideas to decision-makers, to having the courage and skill to manage expectations, give critical feedback, or present what may be unpleasant or unwelcome information to people who hold sway over you. These types of people have a lot of influence over your career success (and day-to-day happiness or stress level), so the idea of managing up can be intimidating.

You know what you're good at, and you know where you're confident. You may be fine talking with peers or people you supervise, but when it comes to delivering an analysis or projection, or presenting to small, senior leadership teams or larger stakeholders, panic ensues. You know that your analyses, projections, and recommendations—while factually accurate—are dry and uninspiring. And if your presentation is dry and uninspiring, *you* can be perceived as dry and uninspiring. You might come across as nervous, lacking in confidence, or even arrogant or pushy, and none of these qualities convey effective (or even readiness for) leadership.

One mistake I hear all too often is that when presenting to more senior audiences, your focus becomes trying to avoid push-back, challenges, and questions for fear that you might look foolish as a result. To prevent that from happening, you give detail upon detail to justify and preemptively defend your findings, hoping there will be nothing left for your participants to question. Unfortunately, this isn't persuasive, it's *dissuasive*—not just because it's distracting and boring, but more importantly because it shows you don't truly know your audience or understand their needs. You think you're being thorough; they think you got lost in "the weeds." You *will* have an impact on the outcome of the meeting...but it might not be the impact you want, and it's all because your word choice, both quantitatively and qualitatively, has missed the mark.

## A.   Relevant vs. Essential Information

Think of it this way. In the diagram below, the large outer circle represents everything you know about a particular topic. This is what makes you the expert on it. It is all important, and influences your perspective, understanding, and the conclusions you draw, so we'll call it "relevant knowledge."

The small white circle at the center represents what your current audience *needs* and *wants* to know. This is what we'll call "essential information." But if you're speaking to your board of directors one day and a group of investors the next, the information essential for each group may change, which is what the other small gray circle reflects. It is critical to anticipate a given audience's needs and adapt your message accordingly. Why? Because everything else that is relevant to you but *not* essential to the current audience (the rest of the big circle) is simply more than they need or want to know, and possibly more than they can process. That's what they consider being in "the weeds," and nobody wants to get stuck there.

**Figure 4: Relevant Information vs. Essential Information**

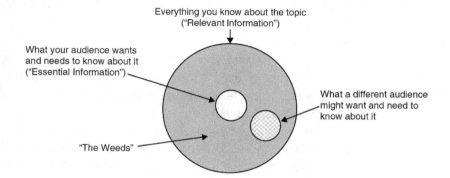

When I share this perspective with groups, I often hear protests that some bosses are detail people and *like* "the weeds." I recommend that you consider senior leaders—whether your boss, client, or a board member, among other relationships—as having the following priorities:

1. Getting through as much as possible and getting out of this meeting as soon as possible.
2. Understanding the content as quickly as possible.
3. Understanding no more and no less detail than is absolutely necessary to answer *their* most pressing "so what?" bearing in mind priorities 1 and 2.

To ensure that everyone is on the same page from the beginning:

- Explicitly state your objectives and end-goals up front. That's your hook. That establishes credibility and importance, and commands the room.
- Then, tell them that you want to respect everyone's time, so you're going to skip over some details, but invite them to interrupt you at any time if they *do* want more, and *be ready* with whatever information you opted to omit. ("Be prepared" is more than just the Scouts BSA's motto.) Most of your audience will appreciate

you being mindful of their crazy schedules and priorities. You connect with your audience by showing forethought, emotional intelligence, empathy, and attention to detail (in addition to simply doing good work). And *that* will have positive influence.

▪ Then, instead of spending your time talking about all the tactical details, be sure to share information that shows you are thinking strategically. For example:

- If you are reorganizing your human resources department, don't just focus on what each move will be; explain the rationale for the change and what the return on investment will be that will make the temporary hassle worth it.
- If you're a tax accountant in a major financial advisory firm, don't just explain to your clients all the details of how you're going to implement changes based on the new tax law; focus instead on the business implications, and how the overall changes will save them money and have a positive impact on the bottom line.

Some of the challenge might be that your ideas may not be embraced immediately, such as, for example, if you determine that the boss's preferred option is not the most cost-effective, or if you have uncovered problems that will require significant changes to be made or that will have political ramifications. This is where it will be crucial to use objective, diplomatic language, as discussed above in Section III.

When in doubt, preface that conversation by establishing shared primary interests, such as ensuring the company is investing its resources with maximum potential return, and avoiding any pitfalls along the route to that goal. This preface will help to manage expectations by framing why you need to share some red flags with your audience, for example. Own your responsibility and your decision, and calmly but confidently make it clear that the biggest failure on your part would be to *not* share your findings. This identifies a clear "why," which paves the way for the audience to be open to receiving the rest of the content you need to present.

## B.  Culture

It's important to acknowledge the role of culture at this point, as it is a major factor in how different people approach the relationships involved in managing up. I've worked with thousands of clients and students, both American and international, many of whom were from more hierarchical cultures, countries, and family backgrounds. For them, the whole idea of proactively asserting your recommendations or contradicting senior leadership—especially in public—is more than simply counter-intuitive.

Individuals from these cultural groups express deeply ingrained values that prioritize showing respect for one's elders and superiors, with strict rules for what that kind of respect should look like. This leads to the conscious and unconscious feeling that it is not their role, as a junior staff member, to tell the boss what to think or do. It would seem overtly insubordinate and disrespectful in a way that would cause great embarrassment to everyone involved, and would be career-ending in their home culture. This leads to an internal struggle of trying to reconcile the cultural values in which they were raised with the professional responsibilities of their current role, as well as with their future aspirations.

My international clients and students often share that although they know, intellectually, that American business leaders expect them to manage up, they have difficulty figuring out how to express themselves in a way that reflects both value sets at once: demonstrating personal authority and leadership skills while showing respect for others in more senior positions.

So, how can you balance these needs, in order to leave a meeting feeling like everyone's needs were met and you came out looking poised, ready, and in control? More importantly, how can you do this without having to abandon or betray a part of who you are, regardless of where you were born or how you were raised?

The first step to reconciling this internal struggle is to remember why you are there. You were given that role because someone believed you were the best person to do the job. You were invited to the meeting because the common understanding is that you *belong* there. People want your insights, not just your agreement. The best contribution you can make is to share information or ask questions that will help your organization succeed.

The worst professional mistake you can make is to *not* share critical insights that could increase the organization's success, or help it avoid disaster. The second-worst mistake you can make is to contribute nothing at all, which simply leaves the impression that you bring no value to the table. A good question is as valuable as a good answer.

Remember that your leadership wants you to be more than a human calculator with a mouth or a "yes-man;" they want you to take on an advisory role. This is not just to make their lives easier in the moment. Carefully crafting your message with the right content, timing, and delivery shows them that you have the analytical skill and the foresight to be able to handle more of these projects. You are demonstrating your own proactive—but still respectful—leadership skills. It's your chance to show them not just that you can lead, but that they can trust you to lead *them*.

# VI. STORYTELLING

Sometimes the most compelling way to convey your point is to illustrate it rather than explain it. This is where the art of storytelling comes into play.

The beauty of it all is that everyone likes to listen to a good, well-told story. A few years ago, I was running a training for a large urban school district. To demonstrate a particular technique, I was reading a short children's book out loud to the attendees, when I suddenly realized Mr. Jones, the burly, fifty-something, head custodian, was leaning against the doorway.

Thinking he might need to take care of something in the room, I stopped reading and said, "Hi, Mr. Jones, did you need something?"

He shook his head with a little smile and said, "No. It's just been a long time since anyone read me a story."

This is the power of a captivating story: It makes you forget what you were thinking about or doing, and allows you to get lost in it, if only for a moment. Persuasive, captivating stories have several key elements to them.

## A.  Stories Need to be Relatable and Inspiring

First and foremost, stories need to be relatable in some way. Even if the specific context or problem is far-removed from the listener's experience, something in the thoughts, emotions, fears, or conversations shared in the story must resonate with the audience. Remember the second C: Connect.

This connection can be made easily through a simple plot structure:

- Start by describing the original state of affairs.
- Next, identify a key problem, and show where things were at their worst.
- Describe the struggle to overcome this challenge, such as competing priorities and risks, obstacles, and ethical dilemmas.
- Then, share the resolution, whether a victory or the hope of a victory, or a failure that your participants want to avoid, ideally combined with a positive lesson, and an explicit call to action.

For people to appreciate where you are, they have to understand how you got there and where you came from. The problems make you relatable, the victories make you inspirational, and the instructional call to action makes you indispensable.

*A client of mine, Malik, was invited to speak at a TED Global conference and asked for my help. His story was incredible: An educated, professionally successful man and a loving husband and father, at twenty-eight years old, he was framed for the murder of his wife, convicted due to a corrupt justice system, and sentenced to the death penalty. He was Kenyan, and in Kenya the death penalty was the only possible sentence for a murder conviction.*

*Talk about a story that's even hard to believe, much less to relate to! But we made it relatable by sharing his thoughts and feelings along the way: Disbelief, despair, seeing no light at the end of the tunnel...and then opportunity, hope, perseverance, frustration, and ultimately, joy and relief upon finally receiving exoneration, a whopping eighteen years later. These are all feelings everyone has felt at many points along life's journey. As a result, while the specific facts of his story would naturally be impossible for most people to relate to, HE was completely relatable as a person, and ultimately, a role model.*

> *And Malik's call to action? No matter how dark things seem, every day, take just one step forward. The connection with his audience was unbreakable, and everyone who hears his story leaves with one thought: If he can do it under those circumstances, I can persevere and overcome my own challenges too!*

## B. Stories Show Contrast

Second, good stories show contrast. It could be a before-and-after example, a promise that something will get better, or a look at two different cases, one that was successful and one that was not. This helps the listener envision both what they want to have happen, and what they do *not* want to have occur.

Albert Einstein once said, "The only rational way of educating is to be an example. If one can not help it, a warning example." Fortunately, both types of examples make for great stories.

Persuasive stories can be real or hypothetical. I'm not suggesting that you make up imaginary clients and situations and pretend that you actually worked with them to turn their business around; that's just lying. But stories can be a way to help your audience envision a possible future or outcome. Imagination is powerful. "Imagine X" is one of the most compelling marketing phrases you can use. Inviting people to imagine or speculate what the future could look like within a particular time frame can help them internalize the possibilities by helping them feel the pain, the pleasure—and the payout.

Fictitious stories can also be a fun way to teach a lesson without sounding like you're preaching. I've run lots of trainings on intercultural communication, and often I'll open with the following anecdote. (cf: *The Big Book of Presentation Games*. Apologies to any insect-lovers out there, but stay with me!)

> *There was a graduate student studying animal behavior who decided to do an experiment. He took a grasshopper and put it on the edge of a table, and said, "Jump!" The grasshopper jumped across the table.*

> *Then he picked the grasshopper up, pulled off two legs and put it back on the edge of the table. "Jump!" he said, and the grasshopper jumped halfway across the table.*
>
> *He picked it up again and pulled off two more legs. He put it back down, said, "Jump!" and this time the grasshopper just inched forward.*
>
> *Finally, he picked up the grasshopper, pulled off the last two legs, placed it back on the table and said, "Jump!" But the grasshopper didn't move. So naturally, the graduate student concluded that a grasshopper with no legs...is deaf.*

On cue, this inevitably elicits a full round of groans and a few laughs. But most importantly, once things settle down, I transition with, "Okay, why did I tell you that joke? Because based on the limited data and understanding he had, the graduate student interpreted the grasshopper's behavior in a way that seemed logical to him. Unfortunately, the conclusion he drew regarding the *reason* for the behavior was wrong.

"In the same way," I tell the participants, "when you have employees, students, clients, or vendors of different cultures, they will occasionally say or do something that surprises or upsets you because it seems disrespectful or inappropriate. But what's critical in that moment is to realize that their motivations or intentions may not be what they appear to be on first glance. It's the *lack* of information you have about their language and culture—and their lack of knowledge about yours—that triggers the miscommunication and leads to wrong conclusions. That's what I want to explore with you today."

Of course, I could launch bluntly into my content with, "I'm here today because you are all interculturally ignorant and biased and I'm going to show you why and how you have to change," but then the listeners would feel insulted, attacked, and defensive. Saying that would create a virtual brick wall I'd have to break through to get them to open up again and be willing to hear anything else I had to say. Instead, the grasshopper story serves as a disarming allegory to gently reveal a primary cause of the audience's challenges in working and communicating with people from different cultures, allowing them to laugh at themselves indirectly and be open to hearing more and changing their thoughts and behaviors.

## C. Stories Establish Credibility

Stories can have a variety of placements and purposes. One of the most important can be as a means to establish your own credibility at the start of a meeting or program.

As I mentioned before, I have led many training programs for school districts all over the country. When I do, there is always one initial obstacle I need to overcome from the start: my title.

Public school teachers can be one of the most cynical audiences to win over. They're under tons of pressure, overworked and underpaid, and most would rather be grading papers or lesson planning (or going home) than having to sit through a professional development workshop run by some academic or corporate type. Whereas in the corporate world my PhD is a marker of credibility and expertise, in the K-12 public school setting, it is often viewed as a marker of distance between my audience and me. If I wanted to have a truly captivated, engaged audience, and make the experience maximally beneficial for everyone, I would have to do some "damage control" as soon as the principal or superintendent introduced me as "Dr. Sicola," in order to redirect their focus and get the energy of the room to flow with me rather than against me.

At that point, as soon as the microphone was handed to me, I began with an invitation and disclaimer: "First, please call me Laura, and allow me to *apologize* for the 'Doctor' in front of my name. After college, when I first started teaching, I was working in a bilingual program in south-central Los Angeles...." At this point people's eyebrows went up a bit, as that's generally recognized as one of the toughest neighborhoods in urban America, and bilingual programs have unique challenges and require unique skill sets in their teachers. That earned some quick credibility and respect points. I had their attention, and command of the room.

I continued, "It was a twenty-four-seven, all-consuming job, and anytime I had to sit in a professional development session run by 'Dr. So-and-So,' my brain automatically went *click* and shut off. All I could think of was, 'Listen, Dr. Smarty-Pants, take your fancy-schmancy research and theory somewhere else. If you aren't going to give me something that's going to make my life easier at eight o'clock tomorrow morning, I don't have time for you." I saw some more heads nodding in agreement. They knew that I understood their challenges and feelings, because I had been there myself. I was connecting with my audience.

Then I drove it home: "So the irony is not lost on me that I'm standing here today with one of those fancy-schmancy titles of my own. That's why all I'm asking is that you give me *ten minutes*, and if I haven't clearly demonstrated by then that the rest of the program is going to give you valuable information and real, concrete, applicable strategies to make your life easier when school starts tomorrow morning, I give you permission to leave, and I won't be offended. Is it a deal?" Framed as a no-lose proposition for them, the rest of the heads nodded in agreement, and a few yesses could be heard. I earned their collective buy-in, and closed the deal.

In all the years I have run those programs, not one person has ever walked out.

## D.  The Effect of Stories

Let's be clear about something else that's equally important: Not all storytelling pertains to heart-felt personal anecdotes or jokes like the previous examples. Maybe you are a pharmaceutical researcher, CFO, or SVP of marketing. Often your product is a spreadsheet or something equally un-sexy. Where does storytelling come in?

Arguably, it's when the data are so nuts-and-bolts-dry (like you'd find in your average Excel spreadsheet), that storytelling becomes even *more* crucial to making an impact. Project what the future might look like if you make Choice A over Choice B. Walk the audience through a day in the life of a real or hypothetical client or employee. You could even talk the audience through what was going through your head leading up to the moment when the big idea came to you.

This is a good opportunity not only to share but to *interpret* the data for the audience. Describe it using some *subjective* language. For example:

- Is it promising, or is it a cause for concern?
- Was the up-tick nominal or critical?
- What *doesn't* the data show and why is that important to you?

Reveal or speculate as to what influential factors might have contributed to this situation, ways it can be mitigated or amplified, and possible outcomes and subsequent effects to be pursued or avoided as desired. Whatever you do, find some way to make it relatable and inspirational.

To be persuasive, at its foundation, any good story needs to be well-written. Whether it's a two-minute story to illustrate a specific point, or an extended story to contextualize and integrate a variety of points, it needs good structure and descriptive language, as is evidenced by any good book, play, or movie script, or even television advertisement. Through that structure, you need to convey two things, whether explicitly or implicitly: *what the listener should think, and how they should feel about it.*

Remember, no matter how long or short your story is, your goal is to use it to *bring your data to life.* Stories not only help the audience focus their attention and connect with your content, they influence the way the audience thinks and feels about it. Stories create inspiration and motivation that allow the content to penetrate and stick, all of which is at the root of influence.

**Use stories to bring your data to life.**

## VII. POINTS OF IMPACT

1. Careful word choice—both quantitative and qualitative—is at the core of clear and effective messaging.
2. Fillers make you sound hesitant or uncertain, which undermines credibility.
3. The right balance of objective and subjective speech reflects the right balance of logic and emotions for each context.
4. Focus on the benefits for the listener up front so they understand the "why." Then explain how to achieve those results through the features.
5. When managing up, don't get lost in the weeds of technical detail. Keep it to strategic, high-level points, but be ready with the details if someone requests them. Be able to separate essential from relevant but non-essential information and adjust accordingly from audience to audience.

6. Consider how culture—including home culture, upbringing, industry, and where you live now— might be influencing what information you or others choose to share and how.

7. When possible, tell a story rather than giving a generic explanation. Use a clear plot with a problem to make it relatable, and a solution to make it inspirational.

8. Stories can bring data to life, provide a non-threatening lens through which listeners can do some introspection, establish credibility, or help the audience visualize future outcomes to seek or even avoid.

9. Persuasive content needs to help the audience clarify both what to think and how to feel about it.

## VIII. BLIND-SPOT CHALLENGE: VERBAL

LISTEN to your recording again, but *don't watch it*, so as not to get distracted by your movements, hair, etc. Don't worry about how your voice sounds at this point. Focus exclusively on *what* you said. Listen and ask yourself:

- Did I use any fillers, excessive jargon, or inappropriate language?
- Were my words appropriately diplomatic, direct, confident, respectful, humorous, specific, accurate, supportive, etc.?
- Did I establish my purpose right away, in a way that was meaningful to my target audience? Were clear benefits established, or did I get lost in features or other technical details?
- Was my organization and logic easy to follow?
- Did I add my own interpretation of the facts in a way that contributed value?
- Did I tell a story? If so, was it effective, and why or why not? If I didn't, is there a story I could have used, and even *should* have used?
- Do my cultural values differ from my audience's values? If so, did I take them into consideration and speak in a way that respects both sides?
- Were my words persuasive? Why or why not?

61

Write down your answers to each question, then consider your blind spot: how many of these answers reflected something you correctly anticipated hearing vs. something you heard (or didn't hear) that surprised you? And does each of those answers contribute to or detract from the leadership image you want to establish?

# CHAPTER 4

## VOCAL

*They were indeed a queer-looking party that assembled on the bank—the birds with draggled feathers, the animals with their fur clinging close to them, and all dripping wet, cross, and uncomfortable.*

*The first question of course was, how to get dry again.*

*...*

*At last the Mouse, who seemed to be a person of authority among them, called out, 'Sit down, all of you, and listen to me! I'll soon make you dry enough!'*

*...*

*'Ahem!' said the Mouse with an important air, 'are you all ready? This is the driest thing I know. Silence all round, if you please! 'William the Conqueror, whose cause was favoured by the pope, was soon submitted to by the English, who wanted leaders, and had been of late much accustomed to usurpation and conquest. Edwin and Morcar, the earls of Mercia and Northumbria—*

*...*

*How are you getting on now, my dear?' it continued, turning to Alice as it spoke.*

*'As wet as ever,' said Alice in a melancholy tone: 'it doesn't seem to dry me at all.'*

—Lewis Carroll. *Alice's Adventures in Wonderland.*

# I. INTRODUCTION

Okay, so now you know what to say. You know how to choose the right words in the right stories to get your point across to your audience. Your facts are accurate and diplomatically stated, you have included the core details and omitted non-essential ones, your story flows logically without too much jargon, and you don't have any fillers. Is that everything?

No—because what that gives you is a great *transcript*, something that looks good on paper. So many people convince themselves that as long as their words are good and their facts are solid, that's all that matters: It's good enough. I assure you, it is not possible to increase your powers of influence by setting the bar at "good enough."

As I mentioned earlier, *what* you say is only part of the battle. *How* you say it is the game-changer, and good voicing is crucial to ensuring that your message lands with the desired impact.

Being able to voice your message appropriately is, by far, one of the most underestimated skill sets out there. By good voicing, I don't mean whether or not you think you have a nice voice. It's about how you *use* your voice *strategically* to help the listener connect with your message and with *you*.

"But wait," you protest. "What if I don't like the sound of my own voice in general?"

Different properties of the voice and different factors involved in the way you use your voice to articulate your message can not only change people's impression of you, but they literally can make it easier for the listener to process and remember what you've said, as well as correctly interpret what you meant by it. The sound of your voice impacts your audience both cognitively and emotionally.

> ※ On the *cognitive* side, the way you use your voice—and as a result, the way your message sounds—will help people focus on, process, and remember your message. This has a direct impact on your image and reputation because someone who can make their point clear and understood is more easily recognized as an expert and as a leader. Naturally, if people have difficulty understanding you or can't remember what you said, it limits your powers of influence.

- On the *emotional side*, good voicing changes how your audience *feels* about you *and* what you said. This is critical because, as anybody in sales will tell you, people may shop based on logic, but they *purchase* based on emotion, and justify it with logic. Of course, there are exceptions to that rule, but the point is that many major decisions are based on instinct...right down to whom people vote for. Once an individual has come to an emotional decision about something, it's much harder to change their mind using logic-based arguments.

**The sound of your voice impacts your audience both cognitively and emotionally.**

That's why it's so important that your vocal delivery is as careful and strategic as your word choice. The way you sound reflects the way you feel about what you're saying, and that has a huge influence on how people react to your message instinctively.

If you are unaware of what your voice is doing, you can send out mixed signals and the listener doesn't know which to trust. This confusion and distrust of what you are saying acts as a filter through which they will process the rest of your message, right down to including decisions regarding how much attention they're going to pay to what you are saying.

In this chapter, I want to show you some of the most influential vocal factors, so you know what pitfalls to watch out for and how to change your mindset and speech patterns to create the impact you want.

## II. WHY YOUR VOICE SOUNDS WEIRD ON RECORDINGS

Before we get into all that, however, I want to demystify something that has probably bothered you for a long time, but you never knew why.

If you're like most people, when you hear yourself on a recording, your first thought is, "Oh my gosh, that's not really what I sound like, is it?" The short answer is: "Yes, that's you."

I do a lot of audio and video recording with my clients, and just about everyone claims that they don't like to listen to their own recordings for a variety of reasons. But whether or not you like the sound of your voice generally, it's true that as you are articulating the words, your voice sounds different to you compared to how it sounds to your audience. Here's a bit of insight as to why, and how to make sure you sound your best, no matter what kind of voice you have.

Simply put, this discrepancy is because you're listening through two different mechanisms. When you listen to someone else, the "input" goes into your ear, hits the ear drum, and sends vibrations through the inner ear canal, which the auditory nerve takes up to the brain for interpretation. This is also how it works when you're listening to yourself on a recording, which is like listening to another person. Think of it as when you listen to someone else or a recording of yourself, you're listening in "mono-sound," or "single track."

On the flip side, while you're speaking, you're hearing yourself in "stereo" or "surround-sound." Of course, your own words still come out your mouth and the sound goes into your ear for the same process we just discussed, but that's only *half* of what you hear.

The *other* half is that when you speak, air comes up from your lungs through your throat and vibrates through your vocal cords, the source of your voice. But then those vibrations also ricochet off the muscles and bones in your throat, mouth, and nasal cavity, and create residual vibrations that hit the bones in your neck and head as well, sending their own pulses to the brain.

It's that "stereo" input through multiple channels that makes your real-time voice sound fuller, richer, more resonant. In other words, listening to yourself through "mono-sound" takes away half of your stereo input. It makes your voice sound comparatively tinny, thin, maybe even scratchy or higher pitched to you, although others generally will not perceive it as such. That's probably why you feel like your voice not only sounds different on a recording, but that on the recording it sounds *worse* than you expected.

What matters most in all of this is that you learn to *use* your voice in a way that ensures that everyone hears your best, most melodic voice. Let's look at some features of your voice, and how to use it in a way that allows you to maximize the fullness of your tone, so the voice you hear in your head more accurately translates into the voice that everyone else hears when they listen to you: the voice that projects confidence, control, poise, and power.

Who doesn't like the sound of that?

## III.  WHAT CAN AND SHOULD YOU CHANGE?

Think of learning to project your best voice as learning to play your vocal instrument with mastery. Of course, if you were born with a clarinet, you don't get to trade it in for a trumpet. I have a relatively deep alto voice. I will never naturally sound like Elmo from Sesame Street—although I could probably do a reasonable imitation of him, at least for a few minutes. On the other end of the spectrum, I will never sound like James Earl Jones, no matter how hard I try.

But in the same way a clarinet can be used to play both classical music or Dixieland jazz, you can also play your vocal instrument in different ways to sound more confident, more relatable, more passionate, more engaging, more serious, or more authoritative. At that point, what's most important is to realize that it's less about whatever "hardware" you were born with, and far more about how you use it.

That's where I want to give you both permission and power: To play your instrument to its fullest range of possibilities, because it is, after all, yours to use as you like. In the rest of this chapter, I'll give you a few "music lessons" to help you learn how to play your instrument in different ways to ensure that the right melody and style comes out at the right time, for the right audience, with the right impact.

Let me clarify one critical point: In no way am I suggesting that you try to sound like someone else; authenticity is key. However, I do want to encourage and empower you to speak in a way that reflects the person you truly *want* to be—you want to have the best version of your voice come shining through, whether or not you believe you have heard that voice before.

Isabel was a client who was frustrated that she wasn't taken seriously because she sounded too young. Together we worked on tiny changes: habitual patterns in intonation, mouth settings, and breath support. We made a variety of audio and video recordings, and what she started to realize upon watching those videos of herself was that even though she may have physically *felt* a bit awkward when implementing each strategy, no change was *visible* to the audience. Her fears of "looking funny" were unfounded.

But more importantly, the person who came through in her videos was still authentic, she was completely herself, but with a subtle shift that carried an air of authority and ease that she had never heard come from her own lips. Isabel saw and heard a stronger, more credible version of herself, which more accurately projected outwardly how she felt about herself on the inside.

In the same way that learning to improve your golf swing might feel physically awkward in the beginning, learning to modify your voice and speech can also feel a bit uncomfortable at first until you get used to it, when it becomes second nature. But once it does, then your ideal voice, your most powerful, persuasive, influential speech style can come through all the time, whether on demand, or as your new default.

That's not to say that you'll win every argument. But you'll know that you sound as authoritative, compassionate, serious, or fun as you need and want to be in the moment in order to be maximally effective at any time.

That's why I want to encourage you to practice all the strategies and skills I'm sharing in the remainder of this chapter and the following chapters to create your "new normal." Take that dusty lump of coal and polish it until you reveal the diamond underneath!

With that, let's look at some of the factors that you *can* control, and strategies to tune your vocal instrument to ensure that you sound like the kind of leader people want to follow.

## IV.  VOLUME

This one seems obvious, right? Just speak loudly enough so everyone can hear you, but not so loudly that it hurts their ears. Nobody wants to strain to hear you, but nobody wants to be yelled at either. Unfortunately, just because something may be obvious or simple, that doesn't mean that it's easy, or that people remember to do it.

This is critically important because it's hard enough to sustain people's attention when they *can* comfortably hear you, even if your material is really interesting. But if they have to work to hear you in the first place, many will soon give up, or they will be easily distracted by temptations like the cell phone in their hand. Either way, your powers of influence are undermined.

That's why it's up to you to do whatever is necessary for them to hear you comfortably, no matter what. When in doubt, *check*. Start by asking, "Can everyone *in the back* hear me?" Even if you don't think you need to do this, do it anyway. If they say yes, you're all set. If not, you need to adjust. You may be surprised how often you hear *no*, so you must *require* an answer to this question. Often people just won't respond and the presenter takes the silence to mean everything is fine. In this situation in particular, silence may very well have the exact opposite meaning.

## A.  When in Doubt, Use a Microphone

One of the biggest volume pitfalls is the difference between how loud you think you are, compared to how loud everyone else hears you to be.

For example, if you tend to get nervous when you're speaking in front of a group, you may not realize that you are subconsciously holding back, and speaking more softly than you normally would. At that point, your volume and hesitation betray your lack of confidence. Don't let your nerves control your leadership image—relax your throat, chest, and abdominal muscles. Open your mouth and speak at a confident volume.

One pet peeve of mine is when I'm in a meeting or at an event, and someone is offered a microphone, but they say, "Oh that's okay, I don't need a microphone. I have a big mouth." Unfortunately, within a sentence or so that same person's volume has slid back into their normal level, so only the people in the first few rows can hear them clearly, while everyone else is straining to hear. As a result, everyone in the back rows is more likely to tune out. (I know I do!)

The choice to decline to use a microphone is half an effort to be funny (with some self-deprecating humor), but it's also commonly reflecting a conscious or subconscious discomfort with using a microphone, and trying to avoid that awkwardness. This prioritizes the speaker's own comfort and convenience over the audience's experience, which definitely does not reflect leadership.

I know a few speakers who deliberately speak in a soft voice because they think it makes people pay closer attention. Aside from the fact that, as I mentioned above, if people can't hear you well they're likely to give up trying to hear you at all, it puts the speaker's ego ahead of what would help the audience receive the message most easily. If that's the only way you can compel people to pay attention, you need to work on the rest of your content and delivery. Do *not* make people strain to hear you.

You never know who is hard of hearing. It's one thing to be aware of it if you're speaking at a retirement home, where you can a predict with reasonable certainty that a significant number of residents will require hearing assistance. But even if you are giving a talk to the young professionals' community network in your city, don't assume everybody can hear perfectly well just because you're talking to a group of millennials.

For many years, I had a neighbor in his thirties, who wore hearing aids because he'd been partially hearing impaired since birth. To look at him otherwise, he was young, healthy, and fit. You would never guess, but if the acoustics were bad, if the volume wasn't up loud enough, if there was ambient noise or music, or if there was an echo of some sort, he often had a hard time hearing what was being said, whether at work or socially.

It's important to be mindful of room acoustics for this reason. How big or small is the room? Is there a lot of upholstery? Carpets, sofas, curtains, drapery, fabric-covered chairs, tablecloths? All of these things absorb sound. You know that your voice is likely to get swallowed up in that room, and it is not going to travel nearly as far as you think it will. Do you really want your impact to be sabotaged by room décor?

The moral of the story is: Just because you can hear yourself, don't assume others can hear you. If you have the opportunity to use some assistance (meaning a microphone), just do it.

**Just because you can hear yourself,
don't assume others can hear you.**

Then again, some people were just born with a small voice. If this is the case for you, it is all the more critical to take steps to project your voice, because there is a common unconscious bias that makes people think that small voices don't reflect a strong leader. Be sure to articulate clearly, as mumbling will make your words indecipherable. Slouching is also your enemy, because it impedes your ability to take a deep breath and get enough air to fuel your vocal engine. When in doubt, stand up, whether you're in a large conference room, or on the telephone. This not only allows you to get more air, but your voice isn't blocked by the heads of others seated around you, since you'll speak over them. If you are on the telephone, people won't see you standing, but it increases your energy level, projecting both your voice and a stronger leadership image, which they *will* hear.

Please see the Appendix section, 'Mastering the Microphone,' for more information on how to confidently and effectively use a microphone.

## B. Audible, Not Overwhelming

On the flip side, some people have naturally booming voices. While talking too softly is not desirable, speaking too loudly can feel overwhelming to the listener, and make the speaker seem overbearing. My husband, for example, is known for his cannon of a voice. When we're in the car together, especially if he's on the phone, I can feel his voice ricocheting off the windshield, and have to gently wave my hand downwards to indicate that he needs to take the volume down a few notches because it hurts my ears.

I had an occupational therapist for a while whose natural speaking voice was piercing in volume and tone, which at times could be physically painful. I literally cringed sometimes as a reflex response to the ringing in my ears. I liked working with her, but was glad it was for a limited time.

If you don't want people to have this type of reaction to you, and you know you have a strong voice or can otherwise become loud and animated at times, be mindful. Keep your energy level in check. Watch people's body language: if you see them squinting or subtly pulling back, take the hint. Bring the volume down.

One way or another, appropriate volume is at the foundation of good speaking. If you're not sure if your volume is comfortable for the listener, *ask*...and not just at the beginning of a presentation as I mentioned earlier. When in doubt, double-check later on. For example, I have heard many people who start at a comfortable volume, but as time goes on they get softer and softer without realizing it. Talk to a trusted colleague or supervisor, friend or relative, and ask them for honest input, either regarding your participation in a specific conversation or event, or for their overall impression of your volume and its reputation. You may be surprised by what you learn!

## V. BREATH SUPPORT AND VOCAL FRY

Remember that in order to buy into your product, service, or idea, people must buy into *you* first. One of the most influential factors in whether or not this happens for you is whether or not you sound like you believe in yourself from the moment you start to speak. If you want listeners to look forward to what you're sharing and to be fully engaged, it's crucial that you sound like you are interested in your own material, and that you're convinced of its importance.

The sound of your voice carries cues with every word, and these cues prime the audience with a sense of how invested you are in what you are saying...and as a result, how enthusiastic they should be to receive the information. Your breath support is a primary factor in this equation.

What does that mean?

### A. Vocal Fry

Think of it this way: If your voice were a car, it would need some sort of fuel in the engine in order to run. The engine is your voice box, the larynx, and the fuel that it runs on is air. When you speak, you need enough air flowing up from your lungs to make your vocal cords vibrate and allow a nice full sound to come out.

But when there is not enough air, or the air is passing through the vocal cords lazily, you won't have your fullest, richest voice coming out. Instead, there's only enough air for your vocal cords to end up banging into each other, causing what's known as "vocal fry."

Vocal fry is that sound your voice makes when you first wake up in the morning, and your voice hasn't really turned on yet. You might describe it as sounding gravelly, even a little froggy. (Linguists refer to it as "creaky voice.") The problem is that when your voice "fries out" during regular speech in the course of the day, it sounds like you're still sleepy and lethargic at best. At worst, you come across as being indifferent or disengaged, as if you have no personal interest in being there—none of which projects leadership.

Note: While we are addressing speech behaviors that result in vocal fry, vocal fry can also be caused by conditions such as acid reflux, or physical nodes on the vocal cords. If you feel like you are physically unable to speak in a sustained, clear voice without vocal fry, consider consulting a speech pathologist, or otolaryngologist (ear, nose, and throat doctor).

## B. The Problem with Vocal Fry

Vocal fry sounds like you lack confidence in what you're saying. The impression it makes is that if you were convinced of what you were saying, you would assert yourself and say it strongly, confidently, and powerfully, instead of sounding like you're holding back due to uncertainty.

On the other hand, vocal fry is something people affect at times, because it has a sultrier sound to it. Think, for example, about Kim Cattrall's character Samantha Jones in the TV show, *Sex and the City*. When she was in her most seductive flirtation mode, she often would fry out her voice so it sounded like a "come hither" purr.

Similarly, vocal fry has become a hallmark of millennial-women's-speak, as evidenced by the Kardashians and other reality TV celebrities. But in truth, it has become a common habit of men and women alike, regardless of generation. While among certain social groups it may be perceived as "normal" in a social context, to others, it leaves a variety of different impressions...most of which are negative, as mentioned previously.

Think back to the original vocal impact goal you set at the beginning of this book. What qualities did you want people to hear in you? What does a leader sound like in your mind? The qualities you listed probably did not include words like *sleepy, lethargic, indifferent, hesitant, uncertain,* or *overtly sexual,* did they?

If not, then what can you do to make sure that your message is conveyed in a way that sounds convinced and convincing? First and foremost, *remember to breathe.*

## C. Contexts for Vocal Fry

A bad habit people often display is what I refer to as "the vocal cliff" where, at the beginning of a sentence, people take a nice deep breath...and start to talk. But then as they're speaking, they start to trail off at the end of sentences. It's not just their volume and pitch that sags, their breath support does too, but they feel compelled to finish their sentence anyway without stopping to take another breath, even though they've run out of air. As the saying goes, you can't squeeze blood (or in this case air) from a stone. The result? They end up frying out their words.

Now, sometimes people do this because they're afraid of getting cut off. Have you ever been in conversation with a couple of 'Alpha types' in a group who tend to dominate a conversation? You may have been afraid that if you stopped to take a breath, someone else would jump in. As a result, you ended up speaking in one long, run-on sentence without even realizing it: The perfect breeding ground for vocal fry.

I'm not saying you should break for ten seconds to yawn, but for the fraction of a second it takes you to inhale, that's not a window of time that would allow someone to register, "Oh, I can jump in here!" If they're going to cut you off, they're going to do it anyway and it's probably going to be mid-sentence, *not* because you stopped to take a breath. For that matter, if someone does cut you off or "steal the floor," so to speak, there's an easy remedy: Take it back! That's no excuse to fall into the bad habit of vocal fry.

Another cause of people falling off the vocal cliff is that they're not mentally present. They're in the middle of making a point, their mouth is trying to complete the current sentence, but their brain has already moved on to what they want to say next.

Again, what's crucial to remember is that the audience is going to follow the speaker's lead. If the speaker sounds distracted, the audience is going to be susceptible to distraction as well. Pay attention. Finish your sentences with as much energy and focus as you started them.

If you started a sentence strong, you're indicating to your audience, "pay attention to this, it's important." But then, if by the end of the sentence you trail off, and sound like you might have changed your mind midstream, what message are you really sending? The sentence needs to sound like the end is as important as the beginning...because, after all, if it's not, why are you including it?

Here are some tips that will help maintain good breath support and a clear full voice.

## D.   Avoiding Vocal Fry

First, like Mom always said, use good posture. Try this:

- Sit down and slouch like a rag doll with your head drooping down. Try to take a full breath without changing your posture. It's hard, and you can feel that you're not getting a full tank of air, so to speak.

- Now sit up straight, look straight forward, and try again. Much easier, isn't it? A full tank of air in the lungs is as important as a full tank of gas in your car (if you want to get anywhere!).

Second, be careful to avoid run-on sentences. If you were writing an email, you wouldn't write one long sentence full of commas and "ands," with just one period at the very end, would you? (I hope not!) In the same way, when you speak, make sure people can *hear* your vocal periods. Keep the sentences at a manageable length. It helps you know when to stop and take a breath, and it helps the listener process what you're saying. Win-Win!

Third, when you speak, be sure to open your mouth and throat. Many people don't realize that they talk through their teeth, without opening their mouth enough to really let the sounds form well. At the same time, they let their throats collapse so the air doesn't have a nice strong track to flow through. Try this:

- Say "ooo" (as in *you*), and purse your lips tightly so there is only a little opening for the air to escape through.
- Now inhale through that same opening. It's hard, isn't it?
- Next, drop your jaw a bit more. Say "Oh!" like you're surprised, and hold a wider, softer opening in your lips.
- Inhale through that bigger opening. Much easier!

Compare the two techniques again. Feel how much more open your throat is, especially if you remembered to drop your jaw a bit the second time. Remember that position when you speak, to allow a nice open "highway" for your voice to travel on.

Fourth, use good breath support. Remember that vocal fry occurs when there's not enough air flowing past the vocal chords to allow them to vibrate fully, and then slam into each other instead, which creates that grinding sound. Good breathing and breath support starts with breathing all the way into your belly (referred to as "diaphragmatic breathing"), not tightening your abdomen in a way that makes your chest and shoulders rise when you inhale. If you relax your torso, when you inhale, your stomach, ribs, and even your back should *expand* and your shoulders and chest should not rise, or only rise minimally after your abdomen has expanded.

Ironically, although everyone has been breathing successfully since birth without ever thinking about it, when many people try to do this exercise and think consciously about how they breathe, they suddenly *cannot* do it correctly, and end up sucking in their abdomen when they inhale, which makes the chest inflate fully and the shoulders rise immediately.

If this happens to you, try lying down on your back. Place one hand on your stomach and the other on your chest. Then relax. Breathe naturally. After a few seconds, you will automatically breathe correctly. You will feel the hand on your stomach rising and falling with each inhale and exhale, respectively, while the hand on your chest barely moves at all.

If you can breathe from the diaphragm in this way, you will have a fuller current of air, which will result in a fuller, richer, and non-fried out voice.

Finally, don't confuse low volume with low breath support. You should be able to speak in a soft voice that is just as full and rich as when you speak loudly. There's no need to fry out your words just because you are speaking quietly. Use the same strategies we're talking about here regardless of your volume.

## E. Speed and Pausing

Next, let's talk about speed and pausing. When it comes to speed, there is a rule of thumb that seems obvious, but is often difficult to execute successfully. The rule is simple: Don't talk faster than people can understand you, and don't talk slower than you need to. Whether you talk too fast or too slow, there are different consequences on the impression you make on others, including everything from your confidence and expertise, to your sincerity and interest, to the audience's ability to focus on your core message.

### 1. Speed Challenges

If you speak too slowly, people's attention will drift. You'll lose your crucial connection with them and you'll risk sounding bored with your own content or uncertain about what you're saying. People can be impatient, and as soon as they feel things start to drag, their first instinct nowadays is to reach for a smart phone to entertain themselves. Once you lose that battle, it's nearly impossible to get your audience back.

However, speaking too quickly can also be your nemesis. I joke with my audiences frequently at the beginning of trainings and presentations that I'm a "born and raised Jersey Italian," which, I tell them, means that I'm genetically programmed to talk at twice the speed of light when I get on a roll. Then I invite them to interrupt me as necessary and ask me to repeat any point more slowly or otherwise clarify it to make sure they didn't miss anything. Then, of course, I have to make sure I keep my speed in check!

There's a time to talk fast, such as when there is urgency, excitement, or enthusiasm. But when you talk *too* fast, you can come across as being nervous, anxious, or in a state of panic. If there *is* an emergency for some reason, urgency is warranted, but when that's your standard speed, it's a bit like crying wolf. If you always sound like everything is urgent, people are less likely to believe you when it is. You undermine your own credibility. Then again, if you truly are nervous about speaking to a particular audience, your adrenaline can make you talk even faster, so it's imperative to make a conscious effort to keep your pace under control so as not to telegraph that nervousness to the whole room. Insecurity is not a hallmark quality of visionary leadership.

The nature of your audience can and *should* determine the speed at which you speak. If they have a lot of knowledge and experience surrounding your topic, for example, you can move through at a slightly quicker pace. But if this is their first time learning about something, you need to down-shift a notch or two. Give them a chance to digest the information.

For several years, I taught graduate school at the University of Pennsylvania, training future teachers. When I observed them teaching in their fieldwork locations, I noticed that a common mistake student teachers made was speeding up towards the end of the class period so they could finish getting through their lesson plans before the bell rang. My feedback was always the same: Just because you finished *teaching* everything you wanted to get through in that hour doesn't mean your students *learned* any of it.

If you find yourself in this situation, go back to the Three Cs: Command, Connect, and Close. The first C is to Command the room, not *commandeer* the room, which is what happens when you plow through your material. At that point, there is no Connecting with the audience, and there is no Closing the deal...only finishing the pitch, which can be both exhausting and fruitless. The needs of your audience must be your first priority.

**The needs of your audience must be
your first priority.**

## 2.   *Lexical Density*

Something else that will help to determine how fast or slow you can talk and still be effective is what is referred to as *lexical density*. Lexical (word) density refers to the proportion of content words to the number of total words in a given chunk of speech. Content words are the meaty words that carry the most information. These tend to be nouns, verbs, adjectives, adverbs, acronyms, numbers, and negatives like *no* or *not*. If a word is technical jargon, you can bet it's a content word. The other words, like prepositions, conjunctions, articles, and pronouns are just functional words that fill in the rest of the context without (usually) introducing any new or critical information.

The point is that the more heavy-duty content words you have strung together in a short stretch of speech (like in any ten-word stretch), the more brain power it takes for the listeners to wrap their minds around it all. That's when you need to speak slowly, to give your listeners a chance for their brains to catch up with their ears and understand what they're hearing!

---

*Let's try these two examples below.* (You can hear them online in the *Speaking to Influence Supporting Materials* page on the website: **https://SpeakingToInfluence.com**)

1. *The more **content words** there are in a **sentence**, the **harder** it is for the **listener** to **understand** what you said.*
2. *The **density ratio** of **content words** to **total words directly influences** the **cognitive processing demands placed** on the **listener**.*

*Even just reading these examples, you realize how much easier the first one is to understand than the second, even though their meaning is essentially the same and you got to read or hear the easy one first, which should make the second one easier. They're both nearly the same length: Twenty-one and nineteen words,*

---

*respectively. But with only six content words in the first, versus thirteen content words in the second, as shown in bold text, the second sentence is more than twice as lexically dense as the first—twenty-nine percent compared to sixty-eight percent. No wonder it took more effort to understand!*

Add to that lots of high-level technical jargon, and the challenge for the listener is compounded that much more. Even reading the above text to yourself silently, you have to read more slowly to grasp the meaning of the second sentence even though it's shorter than the first. That's why, if your speech includes a lot of really dense language, there's going to be more delay between when you say it and when the listener *gets* it. You need to slow down so the listener doesn't feel like they're struggling to keep up with you.

Here's what it boils down to: If your goal is to persuade or influence, you absolutely cannot achieve this outcome unless people have been able to understand your argument well enough to see your vision and appreciate it. If they do not, at best what they're doing is just 'yessing' you. That's not persuasion, and it might even be coercion on your part, or appeasement on theirs. This is not demonstrating leadership in the purest sense. So, slow down. If you want to get your listeners on board with your vision, give them the time necessary to understand your point.

But gauging effective speed is not just about overall pace as could be measured by words per second. Just as any good musical score will have parts that slow down for dramatic effect, other parts need to speed up to shift the energy and the flow. It's the same with speech.

## 3. Pausing

Along with speed, deliberate pausing is a critical piece...it allows your listeners the processing time they need. Inevitably, the last word they hear before you pause is the word or phrase that is going to linger most, letting their brain digest it all before it says, "Okay. I'm caught up!" Pauses also give you a chance to take a breath, eliminate those run-on sentences that confuse the listener, and help you avoid falling into the vocal fry trap.

If it feels unnatural to slow down your pace to the degree your audience might need you to, an alternative is simply to remember to breathe more, to take more pauses, to use slightly shorter sentences, or shorter phrases, and to take more of a break. Now ... we don't ... want ... it to be ... choppy; there's a difference. Pauses have to be in the right place, and at the right time, allowing the words between them to flow.

As an example, over the years, friends have asked me to do a reading at their wedding. One of the most popular wedding passages is from 1 Corinthians 13. An excerpt of the passage is below, which you can also hear online on the *Speaking to Influence Supporting Materials* page on the website: **https://SpeakingToInfluence.com.** If you listen to the audio recording, I'll read it aloud twice: The first time is the way most people tend to read it aloud. The second time, I'm going to interpret it differently, adjusting for speed and pauses. Note that the length of the pauses I'll use the second time are indicated by a single or double slash mark, and any italics indicate when I speed up.

As you listen, pay attention to the energy each time, and be aware of how it influences your experience.

> *04* Love is patient, / love is kind. // It is not jealous, // *it is not pompous, it is not inflated,*
> *05 it is not rude,* // it does not seek its own interests, // *it is not quick-tempered, it does not brood over injury,* //
> 06 it does not rejoice over wrongdoing / but rejoices with the truth. //
> 07 It bears all things, / believes all things, / hopes all things, / endures all things. //
> 08 Love / never / fails.

Do you hear how the first recording feels like it's just going through the motions, saying the words? When it's read like that, the speaker is relying on the meaning of the words themselves to get the message across. But this text was part of a letter that was not just a casual commentary on love; it was an exhortation, an impassioned plea, and call to action. If that's the goal, which version is more persuasive?

Chances are, in the second time around, you had a different experience. You may have noticed words or phrases that you didn't notice the first time around. Something hit you differently. It made you think; it made you feel. Go back and listen again, paying extra attention to where it speeds up, or slows down, or pauses, and how each choice contributes to how the words landed.

Let me clarify, I am not trying to be dramatic; don't forget, I'm not an actor. My goal is to *bring the words to life*. Remember that the word *inspire* comes from the Latin *inspirare,* which translates to "to breathe into," in other words, *to give life*. If you want your words to inspire, you have to breathe life into them. Strategic choices regarding speed and pausing, volume, breath support, and tonality (which we will cover below) are essential to achieving that goal.

> **The word *inspire* comes from the Latin *inspirare,***
> **which translates to "to breathe into,"**
> **in other words, *to give life*.**
> **If you want your words to inspire,**
> **you have to breathe life into them.**

## VI. TONALITY

Tonality is one of those features that tends to fly under the radar, meaning that people don't notice its true power and influential force. But whenever you feel like saying, "It's not what you said, it's how you said it," chances are the speaker's tonality was the big red flag that made the hair on your arms bristle.

## A.   What is Tonality?

Tonality is related to pitch and intonation. Intonation is the movement between high and low pitches. Tonality is the relationship between those pitch changes, including where they occur and when, how frequently, how far apart they are, and the impression it makes. Tonality is the main factor that distinguishes sincerity from sarcasm, for example.

Take two simple words mentioned earlier: "Nice haircut." That can be either a sincere compliment or a biting insult, and the way you know the difference is from the *tonality*. If someone says "Nice haircut!" with an animated tone, it tends to leave the impression that they are enthusiastic and the statement is genuine. But if they drop their pitch so it is low overall and flat with a drop-off at the end, it sounds more like they are scoffing or mocking your new style: "Niiiiiice haircut...." The challenge is that most of us don't realize what our tonality sounds like.

## B.  Monotony

Do you remember the movie *Ferris Bueller's Day Off* starring Matthew Broderick? If not, go to YouTube and look for the video clip of the actor Ben Stein. Stein played a caricature of the world's worst economics teacher. His delivery was so dry that his students were all virtually catatonic. He was the personification of "monotonous" (meaning "one-tone," without meaningful variation).

That hilarious clip demonstrates Stein's character's challenge: Tonality. There was a distinct *lack* of contrast between his highest and lowest pitch. There was minimal inflection or emphasis on any particular word, and the overall range was narrow, low, and flat. That makes his delivery painfully boring to listen to, as there is no vocal interest point. The droning on and on puts the listener to sleep.

What impression does it make when your delivery is monotonous? At best, it sounds like you're going through the motions, with no personal attachment or interest in what you're saying. At that point, if it doesn't even sound like *you* are interested in or present to what you're saying, why should anyone else be present or interested—whether physically or mentally?

Now, while the effect of Stein's economics teacher droning on and on was funny in the movie, it is *not* funny when you're sitting in a class or meeting and your professor or presenter is similarly flat and monotonous. But here's the thing: What are the odds that they woke up in the morning and thought, "Hmm, I think I'll be *really boring* today"? Pretty low, I suspect. But ironically, if interviewed afterward, that same person would likely say, "I think that went well. I was interesting and people were sufficiently engaged." Most people are impressively *unaware* of how they actually come across to others. (Remember the "blind spot" discussed in Chapter 1.) While the presenter might recognize that they weren't completely charismatic, most would give themselves a passing grade (like a B or B+). Their rose-colored glasses (or ear buds?) tell them, "It was fine. It was good enough."

There are two problems with this: First, recall that "good enough" *isn't* good enough if you truly want to engage your listeners and be seen as a leader worth following. And second, even if it *were* "good enough" just to get by with accurate content regardless of delivery style, that performance standard will not propel you to the level of "master of influence."

## C. Tonality as a Tool

Good tonality, in contrast, is not only more *interesting,* and thus easier to attend to, but it's also incredibly important to help people *cognitively process* what you're saying. It helps them both to understand what you want them to understand, and feel what you want them to feel about it.

Think about this: When you were in college, taking notes in a lecture hall, you didn't take dictation, transcribing every word the professor said, did you? Of course not. You jotted down keywords and phrases. But how did you know which ideas to write down? Without realizing it, you didn't simply listen to whole sentences, process all the meaning and then explicitly decide which words were most important. That would take far too much time and brain power.

You see, we don't actually process each sound in order as it comes out of a speaker's mouth. We listen to chunks of speech and our internal radar zeroes in on the words with the greatest emphasis, typically indicated by higher pitch and drawn out length. Tonality acts like a yellow highlighter that catches our attention. When our ears pick up those signals, our brains automatically recognize that those words were important and should be written down, allowing us to process the full meaning of the sentence later, giving us just enough information up front to get it on paper.

Vocal emphasis, or stress, is incredibly important this way. The more strategically the speaker uses tonality, the more dynamic and effective he or she tends to be.

But as the saying goes, more isn't always better. As I just mentioned, *strategic* use is critically important; poorly applied tonality can have counter-productive effects.

## D. Up-Speak

Much to many people's dismay, in many English-speaking contexts in the U.S. and even around the world, some bad tonality habits have become common, both in the workplace and in casual conversation. While acceptable in some informal circles, these habits ultimately can undermine your authority and your ability to positively influence others for two reasons: They *distract* the listener from what matters most, and they're generally perceived as *annoying,* neither of which project the qualities of a leader that people *want* to follow.

One of the most self-sabotaging patterns is known as *up-speak,* or *up-talk.* Linguists refer to it as "high-rise terminal." To illustrate this phenomenon, try reading this next sentence aloud and make your voice go up wherever you see a question mark. You can listen to the recording of the passage at https://SpeakingToInfluence.com:

> *As all of those labels imply(?), it's the lilting, sing-song habit(?) that makes people sound like they're asking a never-ending stream of questions(?) even when they're not(?) because their vocal pitch goes up at the end of all their phrases and sentences(?).*

Get the picture? That vocal upswing gives the impression of you being insecure, implying tag questions like "Okay?" "Right?" or "You know?" But if you were to actually *say* those tag questions every time, it would undermine your credibility. Aside from the fact that it tends to conjure the ditzy "Valley-girl" image of the 1980s, it also seems like you are begging for approval, agreement, or validation on every comment. At that point, it sounds like you are so uncertain of the accuracy or value of what you are saying that you can't even make a statement without checking to see if your listener approves. That is the antithesis of authority and leadership.

Believe it or not, Valley-girl comment aside, up-speak is not just a bad habit among young, millennial women. While there are those for whom up-speak has become an everyday norm, most men and women, older and younger, regardless of race, education, or culture, are prone to falling into that habit at one time or another.

Impossible, you say? The irony is that most people who use up-speak have no idea that they are doing it, but they *can* hear it when other people do it...and they claim to be annoyed when others do!

*A little while ago, I was running a training program for the national sales leadership team of a big tech company. When we got to the part about up-speak, Barry, a successful, fifty-something man raised his hand and said, "Can you give an example of when a guy would do that, because I just can't see it happening."*

*"Give me an hour," I replied, "and if the answer hasn't become clear on its own, ask me again."*

*Later, I had them do some video recordings of themselves speaking in different contexts, and provided guidelines for how they were to evaluate their own performance. As we debriefed the exercise, I asked what people observed in their recordings that surprised them.*

*Once again, Barry raised his hand. Graciously and with a sheepish smile he volunteered, "I have to confess, I heard a lot more 'up' than I expected or wanted to hear, and I realized it was completely unnecessary."*

## 1.   Seeking Validation

Why would someone fall into the up-speak pattern at some times but not others? There are two primary causes: First, as previously mentioned, they actually *do* feel nervous, unconfident, or uncertain about what they are saying (such as when they are giving a presentation in front of high-stakes clients, or when giving an update that they know will make a supervisor unhappy and they are bracing themselves for the response). Even though they may try to mask it, their subconscious betrays them by vocally inflecting what sounds like tag questions, such as "Right?" or "You know?"

## 2.   Mental List Mode

The second reason is due to sliding into what I call "Mental List Mode." Remember when your first-grade teacher taught you to read aloud? She said, "When you see a comma, your voice goes up, and when you see a period, your voice goes down. Let's read this sentence aloud together:

> *"Johnny went to the store and bought apples, milk, bread, and bubblegum."*

On cue, your vocal pattern went *up, up, up,* and *down,* as if to say, *there's more, there's more, there's more...and now I'm done.*

How does this relate to your adult life? You may not realize how often you slide into mental list mode, linking a stream of data points you want to include with a litany of audible commas, followed by the word "and," which serves as a filler. For example:

- You might do this whenever you give instructions with multiple steps, explain something with multiple reasons, or tell a story with lots of details.
- It can be triggered in your elevator pitch as you describe your job and various features and benefits of the products or services you provide.
- It may happen in conversation, as noted earlier, if you are afraid of getting cut off by someone. Perhaps you try to cram all your thoughts into the first sentence for fear that a pause—even a fraction of a second—would be an invitation to someone else to cut in.
- It could even happen at the beginning of a meeting when you're just running through the agenda items with everyone: project update, budget planning, sales numbers, and more.

All of these potential circumstances involve lists. In your mind, each situation involves you presenting one topic you want to share, so you try to recall everything you want to say in a stream of consciousness. All the while, your brain is calculating, *there's more, and there's still more, and I think there's more...and now I've run out of things to say so I guess I'm done.*

Remember, you wouldn't want to read an email that was one long, run-on sentence, full of dozens of commas and *ands,* and only one period at the end. Your eyes would immediately glaze over and you'd think, "How am I supposed to read this?"

That's exactly the same effect you have on the listener when you use up-speak. They hear the equivalent of one massive run-on sentence littered with vocal "comma-*and*" combinations, and only one default vocal period at the end, when you've finally run out of things to talk about.

## 3. The Solution: Vocal Punctuation

Vocal punctuation (including audible exclamation points and ellipses, for example) is as important to hear in your tonality when you speak as printed punctuation is when you write. It helps the listener figure out when each sentence starts and ends, identify specific points, process your ideas, follow your logic, and determine how to feel about what you have said. To project leadership and authority and to be truly persuasive, varied vocal punctuation—and equivalent tonality—is a must!

Let's clarify a technical point: Yes, I did say that one major way to emphasize key words is to highlight them with higher pitch. However, this differs significantly from up-speak. In up-speak, those words—and typically any words at the end of each phrase—glide upwards in pitch from start to finish, regardless of what the word is. But using strategic tonality, the stressed syllable in the word hits the pitch peak, and then the pitch falls at the end.

If we were to illustrate that point, the pitch lines for these last two sentences might look like this:

**Figure 5: Up-Speak vs. Strategic Tonality**

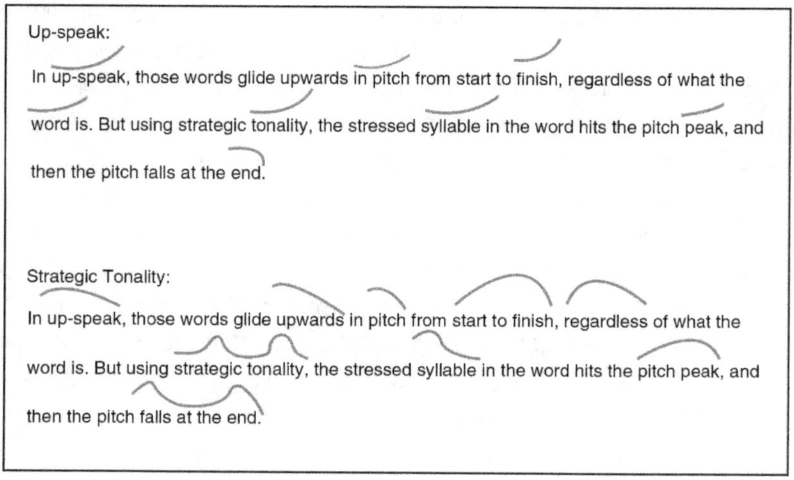

Up-speak:

In up-speak, those words glide upwards in pitch from start to finish, regardless of what the word is. But using strategic tonality, the stressed syllable in the word hits the pitch peak, and then the pitch falls at the end.

Strategic Tonality:

In up-speak, those words glide upwards in pitch from start to finish, regardless of what the word is. But using strategic tonality, the stressed syllable in the word hits the pitch peak, and then the pitch falls at the end.

As you can see, for strategic tonality, the key words do go *up* in the middle, but they come *down* at the end, as does each sentence. That falling, declarative pitch sounds like you own your information, like you are confident in the accuracy and importance of what you are saying. You can also listen to these two sentences at https://SpeakingToInfluence.com.

There's a time and a place to ask questions. But if you want to ask a question, then go ahead and verbally *ask* the question. Don't subconsciously, accidentally inflect it. Choose when you want to make a statement and when you want to ask a question, and make your voice reinforce that choice.

## E.    Building Better Vocal Habits

Building better vocal habits takes conscious effort, practice, and relearning. For example, imagine you are a baseball player trying to learn to play cricket, or vice-versa. Both the batter in baseball and batsman in cricket have to do the same thing: hit the ball with the bat and make it go where they want it to go. But there's enough difference in the details, from the shape of the bat to the angle of the ball and more, that what feels physically natural in one sport feels awkward in the other (as these players' batting averages will reveal). It takes concentration and practice to retrain muscles to be as proficient in the new swing as they are in the old swing.

In the same way, there is muscle memory involved in your speech. To change your vocal habits, from intonation and vocal fry to mumbling and more, you are literally retraining the speech-muscles in your mouth, your throat, and even your abdomen, some of which you probably haven't ever consciously tried to operate. You also have to re-sensitize your hearing to be able to hear some of these destructive habits and their more positive alternatives. But it's worth the effort, because these patterns are some of the biggest factors that determine your authority and presence when you speak.

Try recording yourself and check how often you hear your voice gliding up at the end of a word or phrase, and how often you hear a vocal comma followed by "*and....*" Trust me, you will almost certainly *NOT* hear it *while* you are talking. It's only by listening through the objective lens of the recording that you will get a clearer, more accurate picture of what needs to change, and what is changing. That's also the best way to measure your own progress and executive presence.

## VII. POINTS OF IMPACT

1. It is not enough to know what you want to say. How it sounds is every bit as important in having your desired impact.
2. Your voice affects people in two ways: cognitively and emotionally. It influences what people hear and how they feel about it, which will affect what they ultimately choose to do about it.
3. You may think you sound funny on a recording, but you can adapt your speaking voice so you always project the best possible image.
4. Volume: Don't make people work to hear you. When in doubt, use a microphone if possible. Similarly, don't speak too loudly or people will feel attacked. Volume should be comfortable to the listener.
5. Vocal fry sounds hesitant, lazy, uncertain, or indifferent. Be sure to use good breath support so your words sound full, clear, and compelling.
6. Up-speak undermines credibility and authority because it sounds like you are constantly seeking approval, inflecting implied questions like, "Okay?" or "Right?" Most people do it from time to time, but can only hear it in *other* people's speech.
7. It is absolutely possible to break bad vocal habits and establish good ones, but it takes practice.

## VIII. BLIND-SPOT CHALLENGE: VOCAL

Listen to your recording again, without looking at the video. This time, ignore your word choice. Instead, listen to the *sound* of your voice, and ask yourself:

- *How is my volume? Can I hear myself easily? Does it sound like I'm yelling? How do I feel when I listen to that volume?*
- *How is my speed? Does it plod along too slowly, race through everything, or vary in interesting and appropriate ways? How does it influence my listening experience?*
- *Is my voice clear, or do I hear vocal fry? Do I trail off at the ends of my sentences, especially if they are very long, or if I forget to take a breath? What impression does it make?*

■ *Do I vary my tonality in meaningful ways, emphasizing key words? Do I sound monotonous or disinterested? Do I use up-speak during some or all of the recording?*

Write down your answers to each question, then consider your blind spot again: How many of these answers were because of something you heard that you did, or did *not* expect to hear? Finally, do each of those answers contribute to or detract from the leadership image you want to establish?

# CHAPTER 5

## VISUAL

*'What—is—this?'* [the Unicorn] said at last.

*'This is a child!' Haigha replied eagerly, coming in front of Alice to introduce her, and spreading out both his hands towards her in an Anglo-Saxon attitude. 'We only found it to-day. It's as large as life, and twice as natural!'*

*'I always thought they were fabulous monsters!' said the Unicorn. 'Is it alive?'*

*'It can talk,' said Haigha, solemnly.*

*The Unicorn looked dreamily at Alice, and said 'Talk, child.'*

*Alice could not help her lips curling up into a smile as she began: 'Do you know, I always thought Unicorns were fabulous monsters, too! I never saw one alive before!'*

*'Well, now that we have seen each other,' said the Unicorn, 'if you'll believe in me, I'll believe in you. Is that a bargain?'*
—Lewis Carroll. *Through the Looking-Glass.*

## I.   SEEING IS BELIEVING

There are so many expressions that reflect the value we place on what the eye can see. It reinforces the evidence that if what we see doesn't match what we hear, we are more likely to dismiss what we hear, as discussed in Chapter 2. How often have you said or heard someone say, "Seeing is believing," "See for yourself," or "A picture is worth a thousand words"?

In the restaurant business, there's an expression, "You eat with your eyes first." Whether it's a burger and fries or surf and turf, when a well-plated dish comes out with everything carefully arranged, it instantly increases your appetite. You start to salivate in anticipation of how good it's going to taste.

But if the same food comes out of the kitchen having been hurriedly tossed on the plate, arranged sloppily with sauce splattered all over, you can't help but grimace when you see it. Your reflex thought is, "Do I really want to eat that?"

## II.   DON'T LET THE TAIL WAG THE DOG

It's the same with your speech, and how people listen to you. They're going to anticipate the nature of what you are going to say, and how valuable it's going to be, based on what their eyes tell them—all before you even open your mouth.

The minute you walk into the room, sit at the table, or stand at the podium, people are watching you and your movements, subconsciously evaluating and predicting. The way you look and move will make them either lean in with curiosity and interest, or lean out and brace themselves for whatever they fear is about to come.

Before you get to that point, you have to ask yourself: "How do I want to prime my audience? How do I want them to anticipate what I'm going to say?" When you've decided that, you have to make sure that your visual, physical communication projects that image and gives them that compelling first impression.

I mentioned in the Alignment section in Chapter 2 that body language and visual communication can be the strongest influencers regarding people's impressions of your credibility, and whether or not your audience "buys into you," especially if they distract the audience from the rest of your message.

Let me repeat, it's *not* that "fifty-five percent (or more) of all communication is 'nonverbal,'" as is misrepresented in the myth we frequently hear and see all over the internet. It's that when you are *out of alignment* (meaning when your body language doesn't match your voice or your words), it can seem as though you don't believe yourself. Just as we eat with our eyes first, we also *believe* our eyes first. That's why, if people can't trust their eyes and their ears at the same time because they're getting conflicting signals, they'll weigh what they *see* more heavily than what they *hear* as a result of that disconnect. That *undermines* your credibility.

No matter how much of an expert I might be, can you imagine if I gave a presentation or keynote address and twirled my hair around my finger the entire time? Or if I kept shifting uncomfortably from foot to foot while speaking? Or if I had a hard time making eye contact? You'd likely interpret those habits as a sign of insecurity...or worse, dishonesty. Even if you heard what I was saying and it was great content, you'd probably be distracted by my actions, and then you'd either disregard what I said, or dismiss me as less of an authority, or—more likely— both. Why? All because I was oblivious to the fact that my "message channels" were out of alignment.

Similarly, would you trust your investments to a financial advisor who dressed in old tee shirts and flipflops, or your lawsuit to an attorney who never looked you in the eye, or your physical health to a surgeon who kept biting his nails? I doubt it. Then why would it be different for any other professional who is exerting their influence and expertise?

Let me clarify a crucial point: Your body language doesn't just impact your credibility when you're looking at someone face to face. It is just as influential when you're on the telephone. The fact is that your muscles and the rest of your body are so tightly tied to your voice and the way you articulate your words that people *can hear* what you look like even when they can't physically see you! In other words, your voice and body language tell the truth about how you feel in any given moment.

### People *can hear* what you look like even when they can't physically see you.

There's an expression: "Why does a dog wag its tail? Because the dog is smarter than the tail. If the tail were smarter, the tail would wag the dog." Here's the thing: You need to be in conscious control of your body language, choosing how you want it to reinforce the way your message lands. In other words, you should be able to choose when to wag your tail. When you are not consciously aware of your body language, however, your subconscious will run the show and will control your messaging and the impression you make, often in spite of your goals. The proverbial tail will wag the dog.

So, how can you ensure that your visual communication is always in alignment with your verbal and vocal channels?

When you're taking stock of your physical communication skills and trying to gauge what kind of message to project, there's a simple mnemonic device I like to use as a checklist for my own visual messaging, whether I'm on a conference call, leading a webinar, or on stage in front of a thousand people. It's the acronym P.E.G.S., which stands for:

- Posture
- Eyes
- Gesture
- Smile.

We'll take a look at each of these in greater depth...and if you incorporate the PEGS system into your presentation toolbox, you'll be surprised how much easier it is to make the right impression and have the influence you want to have.

## III. P IS FOR POSTURE

On any given day, whether I'm walking down the street, or standing in a line or in a hallway, I'm constantly amazed by how many people slouch. Necks are craned forward, shoulders slumped, they look sad, beaten down, lethargic. I want to say to them, "Is your day *really* going *that badly*?"

This goes beyond hearing your mother chastising you to stand up straight. The issue is that poor posture implies a lack of interest, a lack of energy or strength, or a lack of confidence, like you're trying to shrink down and be smaller than you truly are.

Some tall women have been self-conscious of their height since middle school when they were a head taller than most of the other kids. They conditioned themselves to hunch down to try to blend in. Unfortunately, that posture habit became their normal stance, and even in adulthood as professional women, that slouch betrays a historic insecurity. Even if they think the insecurity isn't there anymore, it *looks* like it is, and for an audience, seeing is believing.

*Charlotte fit this description. She was six feet tall before she put shoes on, with a robust frame. When working on her business pitch, I addressed her stance and posture. She confessed to having always been self-conscious about her size, and now even more so because she was heavier than she wanted to be.*

*So, I asked her, "If you saw a man who was your size, wearing a power suit and all put together, walk up to the front of the room and stand tall, what would be your first impression?"*

*She hardly paused at all before responding, "I'd think he was in charge."*

*"Would it matter if he was a little overweight?"*

*"Not if he carried himself well, no," she said.*

*"Then why should the effect be any different if the person in the suit is a woman?" I asked. "Own your height, own your size, own your space, own your presence. If you stand there with the belief that you own the room, everyone else will look at you through the same lens."*

*Then I added semi-facetiously, "If not for you, do it for the runts out there like me who would give our eye teeth to be that tall, but can't even look tall when we're in high heels!"*

The truth is that plenty of people—men and women alike, of any height or size—are guilty of bad posture. It's not that you have to stand up, stiff as a board. (You might want to *win* an Academy Award statue, but you *don't* want to *look* like one!) But if you want to command attention and own the room, then you need to look like you believe you can do it.

Is your head angled down, or tipped to the side? Of course, if you've momentarily looked down in contemplation of an idea, or have tipped your head to the side as a result of being particularly intrigued or curious about what someone is saying, that's fine. But when you don't realize that your head is pervasively at a forty-five- degree angle when you're talking to someone, it makes a different impression. It sends a message of uncertainty, which signals a lack of authority. So:

- Plant your feet firmly on the floor.
- Square your shoulders. Pull them back.
- Look at your profile in the mirror (or take a selfie with your smart phone).

Now, ask yourself:

- Is my head sitting directly above my shoulders?
- Is my neck straight, or is my head hovering over my chest, with my neck craned forward?
- Are my hips jutting forward?
- Is my spine in a "C" shaped curve or are my ears, shoulders, and hips in a straight, vertical line?

The difference in your posture is the difference between whether people believe that *you* believe you are a confident leader, regardless of your job title. And the answer to that will determine whether or not they believe in you fully.

## A. Posture's Impact on Your Voice

Your posture goes beyond how you look when you stand up straight. As I mentioned before, your body is directly connected to your voice, which is what gives words their power. When you are slouched over, you can't take a full breath. You can't project your fullest, most resonant voice, and you're more likely to have a lot of "vocal fry" when you talk because you run out of air too easily. It's part of what allows people to hear what you look like. Try this experiment:

- Sit in your chair and slouch, with your chin tucked to your chest, and take a deep breath. Now sit up, with your ears, shoulders, and hips in a column, and your head facing forward. Take another deep breath.

The second breath was much easier and fuller, wasn't it? That's because the second time, your posture didn't restrict the amount of air you could take in, and your airway wasn't squashed, so the air could flow freely in and out.

▓ Now take it a step further: Take out your smart phone and open up your voice recorder app. Slouch down in your chair again, hit record, and recite the alphabet at a casual pace, connecting the letters as you go. "Aaaay-Beeee-Ceeee-Deeee...."

▓ Then sit up straight, take a nice deep breath, and do it again.

When you listen to both recordings, you'll notice that the first time had a lot more vocal fry and sounded less energetic, but the second time, your voice was fuller, you could go longer without having to take a breath, and you sounded more confident.

Even if you only heard a two percent difference, that two percent can be the tipping point in your effectiveness. In school, two percent can be the difference between passing and failing a test. And, after all, Malcolm Gladwell's best-seller was called *"The Tipping Point,"* not *"The Tipping Range,"* right?

## B.   Owning Your Space

Posture is also about how you use your space. For example, if you are standing in front of an audience, whether on stage or at the front of a conference room, do you stay planted in one spot or do you move around a bit?

Some movement is important...it is relatable and engaging, and it feels natural, like you are owning the moment. At different points, you'll want to move toward one part of the stage or room to talk to the people there, and while you're there, plant your feet. Own that space. Talk to those people or address the whole room from that position. That allows you to see different people more clearly, and it gives your group a different view of you and the screen or stage as well. You might stay there for fifteen seconds, two minutes, or more. But own that space. Then take a few paces back in the other direction to give the same courtesy to people on the other side of the room. Again, plant your feet, and own *that* space.

Regardless of where you've stopped, owning the space means being aware of nervous habits like rocking, whether from heel to toe, front to back; or swaying side to side like a human metronome. Shifting your weight from foot to foot and cocking one hip out each time is just as common, but not better. I have a toddler at home now, and whenever I see people fidgeting in their shoes, it reminds me of the universal toddler's "pee-pee dance." I can't help but think, "You really should have gone to the restroom before you started."

Not to mention, if you're on camera, your swaying becomes more pronounced—on screen, your movements are more obvious as you veer from one edge of the frame to the other! At best, your rocking to and fro will just make your audience seasick.

For the record: Some people offer the defense that they shift back and forth because their shoes are uncomfortable or their feet hurt. To those people, I have three words of advice: Wear different shoes! This goes back to the tail wagging the dog: What's the point of wearing those fabulous shoes, no matter how great they look, if they are uncomfortable and force you to move in a way that the *rest* of you *doesn't* look great in the process? If your shoes are sabotaging your leadership image, it's time to treat yourself to a new pair of shoes that are both attractive *and* comfortable.

When you appear physically uncomfortable and unsettled, it projects emotional discomfort as well, which the audience senses immediately. Think about it: Have you ever been to a presentation in which the speaker seemed awkward or nervous? Didn't it make you uncomfortable too? You empathize with someone in that position immediately, and probably feel sorry for them. But that is not the kind of "relatability" you want to establish with your audience!

Ultimately, your posture and mannerisms need to project a balance of confidence and approachability, letting people know that you are in command but that you welcome their participation and engagement.

## IV.  E IS FOR EYES

The importance of eye contact is certainly understood in our society, and the lack of it immediately creates a lack of trust. Once again, if you are clearly uncomfortable making eye contact with people in your audience, whether you are talking to three people or 3,000, the first thing they will notice is your discomfort. If you want to connect, each and every person must believe that you are speaking to them directly, personally. That impression begins with making confident eye contact.

Once, at a networking event at a local sports bar, I met Chad, a financial advisor who couldn't seem to take his eyes off the television in the corner of the room while we were talking. I found it annoying but dismissed his behavior as him being a stereotypical "guy" who had a hard time focusing on anything else when there was a baseball game on in the background.

Against my better judgment, when he followed up and asked to meet for coffee, I agreed. Yet even though we were sitting directly across from each other at a table in a small café with no television, Chad still sat with his legs stretched out and his whole body angled off to the side—a completely disengaged posture—and spent most of the time gazing toward the corner of the room over my shoulder. I could count on one hand the number of times he looked at me, regardless of which one of us was talking.

Needless to say, when we parted ways, I threw out his business card and knew I would never send business his way.

Of course, in a room of hundreds or thousands of people, it may not be possible to make eye contact with everyone individually, but you can be sure to look in all the general sections of the audience, at which point it will appear that you have addressed everyone.

## A.  Gaze

It's not just important to look people in the eye when you are talking, you also have to be careful regarding where you direct your gaze habitually. For example, when thinking about what you want to say, don't glance repeatedly at the ceiling. Trust me, there's nothing scripted up there for you and it's a dead give-away that you're not confident in your message. If you doubt yourself, your audience will doubt you too.

Similarly, shifting your eyes from side to side or looking at the floor projects an air of evasiveness (or even deceit). It can look like you're trying to hide something and can make you seem untrustworthy.

Now, this is not to say that you should stare everyone down. It's not a staring contest, and you're not trying to challenge or intimidate anyone with your gaze. It's a chance to let each person know that you are talking to them, that they are important, and that their experience matters to you. It's an invitation for your listeners to connect with you, and to know that you are reaching out to them.

And of course, be careful to avoid rolling your eyes if you disagree with someone. An eye-roll is an indicator of *disdain*. Whether a roll of the eyes "escapes" without you realizing it, or you roll your eyes, sigh loudly, and throw your hands up in exasperation, a roll of the eyes signals to the other person that not only do you not agree with what they've said, you also don't *respect* it. As a result, it conveys in that moment that you also don't respect *them*. Talk about a one-way ticket to a conversational dead-end!

## B. Eyebrows

Using your eyes to your advantage in public speaking goes beyond your gaze itself. Your eye*brows* are equally expressive and meaningful. For example, when you hear something that is interesting or makes you happy, your eyebrows go up naturally. From that facial expression, people may also—rightfully or wrongfully—infer a sense of curiosity, amusement, or surprise.

When your eyebrows are furrowed down, on the other hand, you look more serious, like you are deep in thought. But that same expression can also make people believe you disagree with what you are hearing, or that you are confused or angry.

I realized years ago that my "thinking face" has my eyebrows furrowed, scrunched down in the middle. I was teaching graduate school at the time, and during office hours one week, one of my students, Sue, came—at my invitation—to get help on her research paper.

She handed me her draft, and as I began to read it, I stopped myself. "By the way," I said, "if you see my eyebrows do this," as I furrowed my eyebrows together and pointed to them, "don't worry. It just means I'm concentrating; I'm not angry."

Sue slumped back in her chair with a huge sigh of relief and exclaimed, "Oh, thank God, I was so scared!"

*SCARED.*

This was a student with whom I had a perfectly good relationship, and to whom I had offered help because I genuinely wanted her to succeed. All the conditions should have made her eager to get my assistance, and had she known, she should have been *happy* to see the expression on my face because it meant I was totally focused on her paper. She had my full, undivided attention. Yet because she didn't understand what my furrowed eyebrows actually reflected, in a matter of seconds, I had *scared* her, and nearly undermined our potential for having a truly open, productive meeting.

The tail *almost* wagged the dog—in other words, my eyebrows started to send a message of their own which was *not* in agreement with what I wanted to convey to Sue. Despite the fact that my initial invitation and overall intentions were positive, my eyebrows had instantly convinced her otherwise. Before I clarified the cue, she had disregarded whatever else she had heard, believing—and misinterpreting—what she saw instead. The reason: I was out of alignment.

Some people are even able to cock one eyebrow at a time. This is usually a clear sign of doubt, skepticism, or incredulousness. If that is how you feel and you want the other person to know it, raising an eyebrow can be a useful cue. If, however, you *don't* want to project that negative judgment just yet, be sure your eyebrows don't accidentally betray how you actually feel, and keep them in a neutral position.

## C.   Eyebrows and Your Voice

Your eyebrows also have a direct influence on the sound of your voice, just like your posture did. Remember the old song lyrics, "The head bone's connected to the neck bone...The neck bone's connected to the shoulder bone..."? In many ways, that's how it works with muscles in your body and your voice.

When you raise or lower your eyebrows, a whole constellation of muscles is engaged, including muscles in your throat that influence your pitch. When your eyebrows are held up, your average pitch is generally higher; when your eyebrows are down, your average pitch falls. This means that, whether a listener is looking at you from across a desk or just listening to you over the telephone, if you want to make sure they hear what you *want* them to hear, you need to make sure your eyebrows are in alignment with the rest of your message.

Try this experiment with the person sitting next to you:

- Have them close their eyes and listen to you say one simple sentence: "Oh, that's what you were planning to do?"
- Say it twice: once with your eyebrows raised as high as they can go, and once with your eyebrows down, like I described above in the story about my "thinking face." (It doesn't matter which you do first.)

- After your partner listens to both versions, ask them to open their eyes and guess in which version you held your eyebrows in "up" position. Assuming you didn't move your eyebrows after you started talking, or just look up or down with your eyes instead of repositioning your eyebrows, I guarantee they will know which was which.
- Then, ask your partner what impression each version made, and how they would feel if they heard that particular response from, say, a client. Here's the thing: Regardless of how they interpreted each—for example, they could have just as easily inferred pleasant surprise or incredulousness from the raised eyebrow position—the fact is that they will hear a different intention along with each version.

Okay, back to our P.E.G.S. checklist.

## V.  G IS FOR GESTURES

Several years ago, I worked with a client, David, on his public speaking skills, and although the story presentation was good, he didn't realize he was a "fidgeter." My mother would have called it "having ants in his pants." As he spoke, he touched his face, folded his arms, ran his fingers through his hair, put his hands in his pockets, waved a hand arbitrarily here or there...it was distracting and made him appear uncomfortable. As a baseline, we did a short video recording of him speaking, then watched the video. Rather than share my observations, I simply asked, "So what did you think?"

David was pensive for a moment, then looked at me, took a breath, and facetiously stated, "I'm going to cut off my hands."

Appropriate gestures are essential to reinforce your message and establish your credibility. Naturally, some gestures are more important than others, and poor gestures can hurt the impression you make as much as good ones can help it. You need to pay attention not just to which gestures you include, but also to the size and direction of your motions and to the amount of energy you use.

## A. Gestures and Meaning

It starts with control, understanding that each movement should reinforce the meaning of what you are saying. Now I'm not suggesting you need to pantomime or choreograph motions to go with each word...you're not playing a game of "Charades." I recently coached Sylvia in preparation for a TEDx talk, and once we started working on the delivery, I realized she had put a gesture to virtually every phrase, which resulted in the talk coming across as canned and artificial, which are two words I would never have used to describe her or her story.

A good rule of thumb is that for speaking, just like in baseball, you have a "strike zone." A safe and comfortable range of motion for your hands is from your shoulders to your hips, slightly wider than your body, and wrist-distance if you hold your arms straight out in front of you.

**You have a "strike zone."**
**A safe and comfortable range of motion for**
**your hands is from your shoulders to your hips,**
**slightly wider than your body,**
**and wrist-distance if you hold your**
**arms straight out in front of you.**

If you were standing in front of a conference room for a presentation to a client or leading a departmental meeting, for example, this "zone" should give you enough space to be able to gesture freely without seeming timid or stiff, or alternatively, without seeming like you're flailing. Within that strike zone there are some important do's and don'ts to be aware of.

## B. T-Rex Arms

First, watch out for what I like to call "T-Rex arms." If you've ever seen a picture of a Tyrannosaurus Rex, you know that they have huge bodies and heads, and tiny arms that don't seem like they'd be good for much in the grand scheme of things. Similarly, when you are speaking—especially when standing up—you might not realize that you have your elbows pinned to your sides with your arms bent so only the lower half of your arms and hands move. It leaves the impression that you are timid or uncertain.

When T-Rex arms take over, there's also one robotic gesture that seems to be repeated ad nauseam: what I call "mushy hands." Pin your elbows to your sides, put your hands out in front of you with your palms facing the floor in a relaxed position, then flip your hands over so your palms are facing up...and then flip them back. I can't tell you how often I see people do this little wrist-flip over and over and over again. It's the visual equivalent of saying, "You know...you know...you know...." It's a half-baked gesture that says, "I know I'm supposed to do something with my hands but I have no idea what it is, so I'll just keep doing this." Does it convey determination, passion, or clarity of conviction? Of course not.

Start by dislodging your elbows and allowing your arms to move from the shoulders as needed. It's not to say that you need to stretch every gesture out to your fullest "wingspan," but the movement should be natural and confident.

## C.   Other Don'ts

Other hand no-no's include repeatedly touching your face or hair, which makes you look nervous, or folding and unfolding your arms, which can make you appear defensive, insecure, or closed-minded. You also want to avoid jamming your fists into your pockets, which can seem awkward.

I once had a client, Matt, who would stand in front of the room during meetings and absentmindedly jingle his keys in his front pants pocket while talking. Unfortunately, people couldn't hear the keys; they only knew what they saw. Let's just say it was distracting in a way that felt both uncomfortable and highly inappropriate. Once Matt was made aware of this pattern, to his credit, he brought that habit to a screeching halt.

If you need to address someone, a positive gesture you can use (whether referencing something they did or said, or calling on them to ask a question or offer information), is to reach towards them with an open hand, palm-up. Rather than pointing with your index finger, which can feel accusatory, the open palm is much more inviting and collaborative.

## D. Head Gestures

Of course, gesturing goes beyond the movements of your hands. It includes the way you hold, angle, and move your head as well. For example, a momentary tip of the head to the side can indicate genuine interest in another person's story, or indicate that you are considering what was said. But if your head seems to be fixed at that same angle for an extended period of time, it can come across as demure, insecure, or even flirtatious.

Other issues with movements of the head can get speakers into trouble too. For example, it can be annoying to watch someone whose hair is in their eyes, forcing them to continually brush it away, or to subconsciously keep their head at an angle to keep their view clear. You can bet that if your hair keeps distracting you, it distracts your listeners even more.

Some head movements have even more severe consequences...

> *Chuck came to work with me because he wanted to improve his executive presence so his top clients would trust him to lead the biggest projects, and so that his superiors would see him as a serious candidate for an executive position. As we talked, I noticed a subtle but destructive habit: As he talked, he kept ever-so-slightly shaking his head side to side as if saying "no."*
>
> *The problem was that "no" was exactly the message he was unintentionally conveying. Whether talking to senior leadership or major clients, regardless of how hard he tried to get his clients to "yes," his body language kept contradicting him, implying, "I don't know," "I don't think so," "I'm not sure," or "That's not right...." Subconsciously, Chuck projected a lack of confidence in his own ideas and abilities.*
>
> *Based on the feedback he received from his clients, directly and indirectly, the response that likely kept repeating in their minds was, "If you don't have confidence in yourself, we don't have confidence in you. Since we don't buy into you, we're not going to buy from you either." In other words, their actions met his subtle "no" with their own big, fat "NO."*

If you're going to plant a thought in people's minds, make it an unequivocal "YES!" Together Chuck and I worked on controlling his motions, training him to refrain from shaking his head back and forth, and instead developing a pattern of gently nodding his head up and down as he talked to emphasize key points and to project an air of confidence and authority. Within a matter of weeks, senior leadership was telling him how much his executive presence had improved...even though they couldn't quite put their finger on why! That's a really exciting kind of influence.

# VI. S IS FOR SMILE

Rounding out our PEGS checklist, the final S is for *smile*. Whether or not you're speaking, your mouth can be very expressive.

## A. The Power of a Smile

You may have noticed that a person's entire appearance changes the minute they smile. Someone you didn't find particularly attractive can smile and suddenly light up with a captivating charm. A smile can also be disarming, and put you at ease in a professional or social situation.

The challenge for many people is that when they're in "presentation mode," whether on the telephone with clients or presenting to the board, they're exclusively focused on what they want to say. They're trying to remember all the important points, not make mistakes, and finish within the time limits. They get stuck in their heads, and they don't connect with their own words, much less with their audience. All of that comes through in their facial expressions.

Not long ago I was working with Simon, a CFO, on his annual report to the board of directors. The irony was that his company had done *great* that year, and he knew the board would be thrilled, but he was so focused on just getting through all the information, he didn't *seem* like he was actually happy with the results he was reporting. As a matter of fact, his facial expressions were about as animated as if he were reading the dictionary. His messaging was definitely not in alignment.

Once again, remember how we eat with our eyes first? Well, if Simon wanted his audience to consume his message and react to it in a certain way, a smile would have gone a long way toward helping them to anticipate loving what they heard. When they saw his serious face tell them that, say, profits had doubled over the last twelve months, rather than, "Woo-hoo, double!" their instinctive response might have been, "Oh... double...is that good?"

Smiling is contagious. People can *hear* when you are smiling. Much like the movement and position of your eyebrows, your mouth shape and position has a physical effect on the sound of your voice. When you smile or frown, for example, a network of muscles influences the pitch of your voice. Of course, this also means that people can hear whether you are smiling even when they are talking to you on the phone...so you can't hide! Realize that your "thinking face" might have something of a grimace, which can make you come across as displeased or otherwise in disagreement with what someone has said. You could end up derailing the conversation without even realizing it.

Remember the experiment we did earlier in the chapter, when you said twice to your partner, "Oh that's what you were planning to do?" Well, do it again, but one time say it with a genuine smile—the kind that makes your eyes crinkle—and the other time, say it with a frown.

Make sure your partner is listening with closed eyes. After you've said both versions, ask them which time you were smiling. Again, unless your smile is one of those fake, stiff smiles that doesn't reach your eyes, the difference each version has on your voice should be immediate and stark.

## B.  When to Smile...Or Not

I'm not suggesting you walk around grinning like a monkey. If anything, habitually wearing a nervous smile when discussing serious issues can be detrimental, as people might think you don't take the situation seriously, or are mocking them somehow. Neither of those options helps you to build the reputation and relationships you want.

The type of smile you give also matters. Last summer I ran a pitch workshop for entrepreneurs. When we got to this topic, one business owner said, "How can I smile when I'm pitching prospective clients—I run a funeral home!"

Funeral direction is certainly not an industry in which clients are excited to be at your place of business. When speaking with a grieving family member about arrangements for their loved one's farewell, it's not a time to tell jokes. Nevertheless, there is a time and a place for everything. For this executive, the end of a meeting with a new family could be a great time for a soft, gentle, compassionate smile to accompany her promise that they have nothing to worry about because she'll take care of everything. That kind of warmth can convey a motherly comfort and reassurance, which can add to the feeling of connection and trust between them both.

One final detail about your mouth. It should go without saying, but I'll mention it anyway: Avoid chewing gum or sucking on any kind of mint or candy when you're speaking. The sound, smell, and movement are all distracting to the listener, plus it impedes your ability to enunciate your words carefully. Slurring or mumbling your way through your point is not going to make your argument more compelling, or project the kind of leadership that will inspire anyone to follow you.

So where does that leave us? As a quick review: In order for you to be credible, your visual communication channel must be in alignment with your verbal and vocal channels. Credibility is the foundation of leadership. And when you are out of alignment, it is rarely just one factor that is out of balance; each channel influences the others. There is something of a domino-effect.

However, when you are out of alignment, your visual channel is the one that tends to be most distracting to your audience, pulling their attention away from *what you say* and focusing on *what they see*. As a result, it is the channel that they will most likely rely on for their final evaluation of your credibility, and on which they make their ultimate decision about whether or not to buy into you overall. If you are authentically in alignment, the audience will not only hear what you say, but will know what you genuinely think and how you feel about it, and *that* is the most powerful part of your message.

## VII. POINTS OF IMPACT

1.  If what people hear, verbally and/or vocally, does not fit with what they see, they are far more likely to believe their eyes and disregard their ears.
2.  The acronym P.E.G.S.—**P**osture, **E**yes, **G**estures, **S**mile—can serve as a checklist to ensure your visual channel stays in alignment, and

that you physically project your best leadership image whenever you need to speak to someone.

3. Posture is about how you own your space. It influences your vocal delivery as well, whether you are sitting or standing.

4. Eye contact (or lack thereof), eye movement, and even your eyebrows all convey messages. Eyebrow movement affects your vocal delivery.

5. Gestures can be made with your hands, head, shoulders, and more.

6. Smiling is important...as is what kind of smile to give, and when *not* to smile. Smiling (or not) also influences your vocal delivery. A smile that includes the eyes (a sincere smile) sounds different than a perfunctory, half-hearted one.

## VIII.   BLIND-SPOT CHALLENGE: VISUAL

This time, *watch* your recording again, but on *mute*. Do not listen to the video. As you watch, use the P.E.G.S acronym as a checklist and ask yourself:

- **P** - *How is my* **posture**? *Do I look poised and confident, or am I shifting from foot to foot, wiggling, or otherwise hunched over or even too rigid or straight?*

- **E** - *What am I looking at? Are my* **eyes** *shifting all around, or am I making eye contact (with the camera lens)? Do I constantly look up at the ceiling as I try to remember what to say? What about my eyebrows? Are they expressive, and if so, is it in a good way?*

- **G** - *Do I* **gesture**, *or am I immobile the entire time? Does my head wobble around or move in a subtle but interesting way? Do I shrug my shoulders? What are my hands doing? Do they seem to reinforce the point I'm making, or are they repetitive, timid, or all over the place?*

- **S** - *Do I* **smile** *when I should, or otherwise vary my facial expressions in a way that matches the feeling behind what I'm saying? Do I look like I mean what I say? Or is my face an emotionless mask the entire time?*

Write down your answers to each question, then consider your blind spot again: How many of these answers reflected what you expected to see, vs. what you did *not* expect? And do each of those answers contribute to or detract from the leadership image you want to establish?

# CHAPTER 6

## AUTHENTICITY AND INFLUENCE

*'Who are you?' said the Caterpillar.*

*This was not an encouraging opening for a conversation.*

*Alice replied, rather shyly, 'I—I hardly know, sir, just at present—at least I know who I was when I got up this morning, but I think I must have been changed several times since then.'*

*'What do you mean by that?' said the Caterpillar sternly. 'Explain yourself!'*

*'I can't explain myself, I'm afraid, sir,' said Alice, 'because I'm not myself, you see.'*

*—Lewis Carroll. Alice's Adventures in Wonderland.*

## I.   THE IMPORTANCE OF AUTHENTICITY

Let's recap: We've just done a deep dive into understanding the little details that make a huge difference in the impressions we make and the responses we get. We explored what it is about the alignment of our verbal, vocal, and visual communication that sometimes—unbeknownst to us—projects an image that goes *against* the impression we want to make. And we looked at ways to change that impression for the better, such as avoiding fillers, remembering to use "vocal periods" (allowing your pitch to drop to indicate the end of a sentence), or improving your posture, just to name a few.

Nevertheless, while these are all skills you can develop, in order to truly establish the credibility you need to get the results you want, there's one more piece you need to perfect. You—and your presentation—have to feel and appear *authentic*.

## II. BALANCING AUTHENTICITY AND EFFECTIVENESS

If you want to influence the way other people think, the decisions they make, the actions they take, and the motivation that drives them, *authenticity is a fundamental prerequisite*. People can sense a fake much the same way dogs can smell fear. When they sense that something is inauthentic, it undermines the persuasive power of your argument.

But authenticity alone doesn't guarantee effectiveness. It *is* possible to be totally authentic but still be ineffective. For example, if your boss or significant other makes a decision that makes you, in every fiber of your being, want to jump up and say, "Are you kidding me? That's the stupidest thing I ever heard!" it would be *authentic* for you to express that sentiment. But, it would also probably be career- or relationship-suicide. If you want to be *effective* in having them be open to listening to your ideas and adjusting their plans and behavior accordingly, you have to figure out how to be authentic in the appropriate way in each situation.

But how can you do that when you are dealing with different groups that may have different priorities, appreciate different types of information, or recognize different characteristics as being desirable or relatable? This is a nearly universal challenge, and one of the most frequently cited internal challenges voiced by many women and minorities I work with. When working with people who don't think, act, or even look like you, what does "effective authenticity" look and sound like?

When we think about this, it's easy to let all sorts of "head trash" get in the way. We tend to place limitations on ourselves. We see a fool's choice, a false set of two (and only two) options: That with some audiences, we can *either* be authentic *or* effective, but not both. This fool's choice is not only an erroneous assumption, it's a self-destructive one. The truth is that, in just about any context, you should be able to be yourself *and* be at your best *and* be compelling and persuasive, all at the same time.

Of course, trying to do this can be anxiety-producing when managing up or speaking in front of high-stakes audiences such as major clients, business prospects, or the board of directors. There is often a conscious or subconscious fear that you have to prove yourself: prove that you are smart, that you have done the work, even that you belong there.

At its worst, this is known as the "imposter syndrome," which is the fear of being exposed as a fraud, even when deep down, you know you aren't. This false belief is self-destructive, because ironically, it becomes a self-fulfilling prophecy. If you assume that you cannot be true to your authentic self and still be accepted, you end up holding back, or otherwise trying too hard to be someone you're not. That comes across as a lack of confidence, which makes people believe you don't belong there after all! Now what's the use of that?

Ultimately, people need and want the real you to shine through. Transparency and even a bit of humility is crucial to establishing trust and credibility. The question then becomes *how* to truly be yourself and share your feelings, experiences, thoughts, ideas, and personality in a way that lets people see who you really are, and to do so in a way that resonates effectively with them.

So how can you balance authenticity with effectiveness? That is what the rest of this chapter is going to explore. It all starts with a critical mindset shift.

## III.  SPEECH STYLE AND IDENTITY

This shift can be challenging because although it's something most people don't consciously think about, a big part of how they identify themselves is anchored in how they talk. For example, as soon as you hear someone with an accent that's different from yours, you immediately feel a sense of "other." Alternatively, if you are traveling to another region of the country or abroad and are used to sounding different from everyone else, when you unexpectedly *do* hear someone who sounds like you, you feel an immediate connection with that person. Your instinct is to think, "Oh, you're like me! We have something in common." There's a comforting sense of connection.

Whether it's the kinds of wording you use, your pronunciation, or your body language, all these cues serve as markers that indicate something about your personality, where you are from, your heritage, your education, or other factors related to who you are. These are wonderful things to be proud of.

As I mentioned before, I grew up in a primarily Italian-American family in New Jersey, and there was no question that we gestured a lot when we talked, especially when things got animated. We used to joke that if you wanted one of us to keep quiet you'd have to make that person sit on their hands! Family members, friends, and classmates who shared a similar heritage all recognized the same habit in themselves. We'd laugh about it together, and it strengthened our connection.

I first became aware that I had an accent (spoiler alert: so do you and so does everyone; there's no such thing as speaking "without an accent") when I was a freshman in college. I attended American University in Washington, DC, and the other students in the dormitory were from all over the country. I realized that my friends took great joy in asking me what I was drinking, in hopes it was coffee. It took me the longest time to realize that they thought it was hilarious that I pronounced it "cua-fee" instead of "cah-fee" like most of them did. What sounded completely normal growing up in New Jersey sounded funny and foreign once I was out of state, but it served as a clear marker of a part of my identity. Nevertheless, after a while I got tired of the joke, so I decided to remove the target: I learned to pronounce it "cah-fee" to blend in better so it wouldn't always be such a distraction to others and they'd stop mentioning it!

I had a valid reason for making this decision, but it begs the question: If I changed the way I spoke, was I trying to act like someone I'm not, or otherwise change my identity? Was it possible to reconcile the need to be accepted by another group while still having a sense of personal integrity and authenticity? If so, how?

The good news is that it is absolutely possible to do both: To be true to yourself and your identity but also to grow and *expand* that sense of identity to allow you to be more effective in ever-wider circles. But in order to do so, you have to stop thinking in "black-and-white" terms.

## A.  Monochromatic Thinking

When thinking about identity, we like to define our identities in certain categories. For example, I'm Italian-American, a first-born child, a published author, a TEDx speaker, a coach, a woman, a business owner, and a mother. We all take pride in sharing some common traits with other people who identify as being part of one or more of our same groups.

At the same time, however, along with category labels come stereotypes, for better or for worse. Like it or not, people jump to certain conclusions about us based on our communication style, ranging from assumptions about our intelligence and likability to our professional capabilities and trustworthiness. And we can get annoyed when people make assumptions about us, especially if those assumptions aren't flattering. It's like they put us in a box limited by stereotype, and underestimate us because of our role, education, age, gender, rank, or color.

But ironically, we do that to *ourselves* each time we resist learning to adapt our speech style by uttering the phrase, "That's not me." When we say that, what we are also implying is that something else *is* me, and that those boundaries are finite and unchanging. It's what I call "monochromatic thinking," where everything is black and white: "This is my box, that is your box. This one is me, that one is not me." But with that fixed view of yourself and your identity, you limit your true potential to have a greater impact on more people.

For example, when I look back on my life, thirty years ago, I spoke only English; that was me. I didn't speak Spanish or Japanese. That *wasn't* me then, but it is now. Twenty years ago, when I graduated from college, I swore I would *never* go to graduate school. That was *definitely* not me; I was sick of being a student. Well, a teaching credential, Master's degree, and PhD later, I have finally accepted the fact that, yes, I guess grad school *was* me after all.

Ten years ago, I didn't think I'd ever own a business. That wasn't me because I thought I wanted to be a tenured professor. At least, that was *supposed* to be me...(Are you noticing a pattern here?) And as recently as a couple of years ago, I wasn't a mother. That wasn't me. But now I have a two-year old son and a sixteen-year-old stepson at home. Being a mom *is* me, in wonderful ways I never could have imagined.

But as each of these opportunities presented itself, I not only learned to walk the walk; I had to learn to talk the talk required for me to be successful in that new role. I learned the expectations, cultural protocols, and even national language needed to live and work in Japan. I learned to think and speak like a researcher while earning my doctorate. I learned to negotiate contracts in building my business. And I learned that no matter how eloquent and logical you can be academically and professionally, you will never win an argument with an infant.

Do you know what the best part is? I *like* all these new parts of myself. I've learned to expand my sense of identity to incorporate each of these new elements and communication styles, without sacrificing any other parts of myself to make room for them. I turn them on or off whenever I want. I own them. I can speak in Japanese when I go to Japan, and switch back to English when I return to the U.S. I can speak "research-ese" when I am presenting at an academic conference, talk in business terms when working with corporate and government clients, and even talk a little baby-talk when I'm at home.

That's why I learned to say "cah-fee" as my "new normal" at school, and when I was back home with my family and friends, I'd revert back to saying "cua-fee." I still do, and now both feel authentic. I don't feel like I am betraying my heritage, I just want to control what captures people's attention, and ensure they are focusing on what *I* want them to focus on, rather than on extraneous details, so I can get the response I want.

## B.  Prismatic Voice

For you to get the result you want from any given engagement, it's all about knowing who will respond best to which speech style, in which context. Does the situation require more directness, or more diplomacy? More patience, or more efficiency? Should you use lots of technical jargon and acronyms, or stick with day-to-day words? Is it time for a reprimand or a pep-talk? Should you offer a handshake or a hug?

Some people might resent you or be intimidated if you barked orders in the office, while barked orders on the football field or battle field will make others feel safe and confident that they know exactly what's expected of them.

And while expanding our identity is important, the beauty is that at the same time, most people don't even realize what a wide range of speech styles they already have at their disposal, *naturally*. I saw the most innocent, naturally occurring example of this one day in my own house about a year ago shortly after my son, Dante, was born. I was sitting on the couch with my two boys, and Thomas, my teenager, was playing with the baby, saying things like, "Hi there! How's my baby brother? I missed you!" in a sing-song voice. Suddenly he stopped, looked at me and said, "Why can't I ever talk to him in a normal voice? I can't just look at him and say, 'Hey, how's it going?' It doesn't work!"

Up until a few months earlier, I don't think that voice had ever come out of Thomas, at least, not for any extended period of time. But for him, this was a completely natural, *unplanned* shift. It just came out of him like that. It felt like the right thing to do at the time, given whom he was talking to. And when his baby brother flashed him that big, toothless grin in return, it confirmed what his instincts were telling him: That sing-song voice was the best way to get the desired response from his audience.

Thomas was able to do this authentically and effectively because we all have what I like to call a *"prismatic voice."* It's like when white light passes through a prism and on the other side it breaks into all the colors of the rainbow. In the same way, *you* are white light, and within you are an infinite variety of colors, shades, and tints. When you enter the "prism" of a particular situation, the key is to determine which of your colors needs to shine most brightly to get the desired response.

This is 100 percent as relevant in professional situations as it is in personal ones.

---

*A little while ago, I had a conversation with Mandy, an African-American woman, maybe in her late forties. She shared that whenever she had to give a presentation to senior leadership, most of whom were older white men, she felt like she had to speak precisely, and enunciate her words carefully, because she didn't want to get pigeon-holed into some ethnic stereotype because of how she talked. At the same time, however, she also worried about whether or not she was really being herself.*

*So, I said, "Let me ask you a question. Do you have any kids?"*

*"Yes," she said, "I have a twenty-year-old son."*

*"Got it," I said. "Now, I don't want to make any assumptions, but, he's black too, right?"*

*She laughed. "Yes, he is."*

*"Okay, just checking. So, have you ever had a conversation with your son that sounded something like this: (over-articulating*

---

*every syllable for emphasis) I-want-you-to-listen-to-me-very-carefully-because-I-am-only-going-to-say-this-once.   Are-you-paying-attention?"*

*She laughed again and said, "You mean, today? Yes, I've definitely said something like that plenty of times."*

*"Okay," I said, "then let me ask you this: When you have that conversation with him...are you 'talking white?'"*

*She stopped and looked at me for a moment. "No."*

*"Good. Then I want you to look at it this way: When you're speaking with the executive group, consider that you're actually reaching into your 'mom' tool box, borrowing one of the tools—that of more precise articulation—and applying it in this new context, where you also feel like it is in your best interest to pronounce things more deliberately, for whatever reason. But know that from the beginning, that strategy has always been an authentic part of you."*

*That's when I explained to her how her prismatic voice works. "Maybe your typical 'mom' style is a nice sunny yellow, and your default professional work style is your green. But you also have a more 'take charge' style...let's call it your 'red.' It comes out a little clearer, firmer, sometimes a bit more staccato. So just like those times when you feel like you need to be more 'red' with your son, at work, when you want to ensure your message is heard in a certain way, you can reach into that same red to borrow some of its components, like enunciating more carefully. But maybe leave out the pointed index finger and the facial expression that implies, 'Boy, if you know what's good for you, do not make me say this twice!'"*

Ultimately, the choice of what to borrow and how to apply it is totally up to you because it's already part of your prismatic voice, part of your repertoire, 100 percent authentically you.

You see, at its core, the key to effective communication is learning to speak in a way that lets your audience process the content of your message easily, without getting distracted by something in the delivery. And you absolutely *can* do that while being true to who you are.

That's why, when thinking about what to adjust and whether or not to adjust it at any given moment, there's really only one critical question that we need to ask: "To what extent is this aspect of my speech style distracting my audience from understanding what I want them to understand, and keeping me from having the impact I want?"

**"To what extent is some aspect of my speech style distracting my audience from understanding what I want them to understand, and keeping me from having the impact I want?"**

Think back to our Verbal-Vocal-Visual diagrams in Chapter 2. When your listener perceives you to be *out of alignment*, the factor they find to be the most distracting will be the biggest influence in how they negatively evaluate your credibility. That's really the key to deciding whether it makes sense for you to expand your speech repertoire by including details that are more relatable to your target audience and incorporate them into your identity.

The more easily you learn to shift naturally and comfortably from one style to another, the greater will be your ability to get through to more people and expand your sphere of influence. This is known as "code switching."

## C.   Code Switching

Code switching refers traditionally to switching from one language to another, such as Spanish at home but English at work, or English to coworkers then Mandarin when a client from Beijing calls on the phone. It can also mean switching mid-story or mid-sentence, if you and the other person are both bilingual, perhaps because it's easier to explain a concept in one language than another, or perhaps you want to make a momentary joke like a pun or shared cultural reference that wouldn't translate well into the other language. For our purposes, however, the "code" isn't so much which language we speak, but what style, register (i.e., level of formality) or variety of that language we use at any given moment. It's often more about making subtle adjustments to meet the expectations and needs of a particular listener or audience.

For example, if you're at work and you're explaining something exciting to other experts in your same field, you can be as technical as you want, use as much jargon and as many statistics and measurements as necessary, and know that it is expected and appreciated. But when you get home at the end of the day and your significant other asks how your day went, when telling them about the same exciting development, you won't likely tell the story in the same way. You'll probably use simpler language, go into far less detail, and explain the big picture in general terms. It's not with the intent of being disrespectful to your significant other; if anything, they will appreciate your sparing them the excessive technical minutiae, which they wouldn't have understood or cared about anyway.

Now, if your child asked you the same question, you'd change your approach again, and explain that mommy or daddy had a big meeting today with some important people, and it was hard but you did your best, and they decided that your idea was the best one. In the end, everybody was happy so you had a good day.

But chances are, it's not just about the type of language you used. You probably even changed the way you used your voice. When talking to your young child, you may have told a story a bit slower, you might have used a more dramatic or sing-song inflection in your voice to make it sound really important or really interesting. The point is that you instinctively know that for the other person to relate to you and be able to connect with your story, you need to adjust somehow. It is a great skill to have to be able to switch deftly and on command, but sometimes there can be a rather steep learning curve as you expand your communication skills to incorporate the new "code."

In the beginning, it may not be easy and it may take you some time to get comfortable with the new code. It's also possible that it may never feel *as* natural or be *as* effortless to communicate in that second language or style as it is in the first. Often it will be, but either way, you still have that invaluable resource available to you. That skill is there for you to tap into whenever you want.

I first wanted to learn Spanish when I was little, maybe four or five years old. My non-Italian grandmother is from Chile, and she would come to visit at Christmas. I remember watching her on the telephone talking with her siblings back in Santiago and using this "secret language" (known to the rest of the world as Spanish) that I couldn't understand. It was the coolest thing in the world, and I was green with envy that I couldn't participate. I'd never known anyone else who was bilingual, and I wanted so badly to be part of that inner circle of people who could speak and understand it, not be left out of the circle, forever wondering what they were saying.

That was the first goal that I remember ever setting for myself, at five years old. I wanted to have the same superpower that Grandma had and be able to switch back and forth from my language, which was English, to that secret code language that Grandma could speak.

Now fortunately, over the course of the next fifteen or twenty years, I was able to do that. Today, my Spanish is good (even if not native-like). But I still have the occasional opportunity to work with Spanish-speakers socially, professionally, or otherwise and can tap into that resource, whenever it makes sense to do so. Maybe they actively need me to do so because my Spanish is better than their English, or because it just helps them to feel more connected with me if I slide into Spanish for a few sentences here and there.

The value is that it lets them know that I have put in a similar effort to learn Spanish that they have put in to learning English. There is suddenly an understanding, a mutual appreciation, a mutual respect. By switching into that world, suddenly, there is a deeper connection and a bonding that occurs which deepens trust and makes all communication much easier.

Speaking in Spanish will never be as comfortable as speaking in English is for me, but now it is an authentic part of who I am, which I can turn on and turn off at will, to have the impact I want.

Throughout life you'll need to learn to use all sorts of different codes, and be able to identify the times when you should and should not use them. Sometimes, this is the hardest part. For example, I spent years learning to speak the language of academia as a PhD student, and no sooner had it finally become second nature to me, than I had to *unlearn* it when I started doing corporate consulting and coaching. In this new context, "professor-speak" was too heady, dense, and abstract for professionals who were more interested in the practical application of my work than all the theory behind it. I was in danger of triggering those ivory-tower stereotypes of people who have all sorts of theories but no clue about the "real world." I was not relatable to my new audience.

It's one thing to want to sound smart, but it's crucial to do so in a way that does *not* make the audience feel dumb! You don't want to be so technical that your explanation goes over their heads. If they finish listening to you and their internal reaction is, "I have no idea what you just said," it doesn't matter how "smart" you sounded, because you missed the mark.

Don't get me wrong—I'm not saying that you have to "dumb it down." The content of your message still has to be every bit as valid and insightful, but sometimes you have to ratchet down the formality and technical jargon a couple of notches to make it digestible.

Code switching even applies when you're talking across functions within a company. Whether you're an IT expert who has to explain to business development people why a new piece of software architecture is needed, or you're in marketing and need to persuade the finance team to increase your budget, it's the same principle. The goal is to convey your expertise in a way that makes it so easy for the listener to just *get it* that you make *them* feel smart just listening to you! That will make them think you are smart as a result, and *that's* persuasive. But the only way to do that is to learn to speak in a way that makes sense to them. That's where you make real connections, and real progress...and get real results.

## IV. POINTS OF IMPACT

1. Regardless of how you adjust your speaking style to meet the needs of a particular audience or context, it must come across as authentic, or you will undermine your own powers of influence.
2. Monochromatic thinking, i.e., "This is me; that's not me," is self-limiting. Your identity is flexible, and if you want your sphere of influence to expand, allow your sense of identity to expand accordingly, in order to learn and incorporate new communication styles.
3. Your Prismatic Voice is one of your greatest assets. Recognize how you speak naturally in different ways to different people,

and learn to shift freely from one "color" to another as it will best benefit you in the moment.

4. Code switching is the practice of switching speech styles, and the skill set that will allow you to leverage all the colors of your Prismatic Voice to your greatest advantage.

# V. BLIND SPOT CHALLENGE: AUTHENTICITY

Reflect back on the scenario you chose for your video. Analyze the context:

- To whom were you talking? Where would that conversation have taken place? When and why?
- What mood or mindset would the listener (probably) have been in at the start? What mood or mindset would you have wanted them to be in when you finished?
- What qualities or characteristics do they value and respect? What qualities would they need to see in you to be most receptive to your message? Give that set a color. (For example, call it "orange.")

Now do some introspection:

- Do you feel like those qualities naturally describe you? If not, think about a time when you *did* demonstrate some "orange" naturally, even if in a very different context, in a way that feels authentic to you. (I guarantee it has happened at least once in your life!)

Go back and watch your video again with the sound turned on.

- Did you see any "orange" coming through? How? If not, why?
- When you first made the recording, did you think that ultimately you projected more "orange" than you ultimately saw in the video, less, or the same amount?
- What would you need to do differently to be more *authentic and effective*?

Write down your answers to each question, then consider your blind spot again. How many of these answers contribute to or detract from the leadership image you want to establish?

# CHAPTER 7

## INFLUENCE IN CONTEXT

*'Please come back and finish your story!' Alice called after it...but the Mouse only shook its head impatiently, and walked a little quicker.*

*'What a pity it wouldn't stay!' sighed the Lory, as soon as it was quite out of sight....*

*'I wish I had our Dinah here, I know I do!' said Alice aloud, addressing nobody in particular. 'She'd soon fetch it back!'*

*'And who is Dinah, if I might venture to ask the question?' said the Lory.*

*Alice replied eagerly, for she was always ready to talk about her pet: 'Dinah's our cat. And she's such a capital one for catching mice you can't think! And oh, I wish you could see her after the birds! Why, she'll eat a little bird as soon as look at it!'*

*This speech caused a remarkable sensation among the party. Some of the birds hurried off at once...On various pretexts they all moved off, and Alice was soon left alone.*

*'I wish I hadn't mentioned Dinah!' she said to herself in a melancholy tone. 'Nobody seems to like her, down here, and I'm sure she's the best cat in the world!'*

*—Lewis Carroll. Alice's Adventures in Wonderland.*

## I.   THE PLACE AND TIME FOR INFLUENCE

Where do you need to be influential? This is a point that just about everyone overthinks. The fact is, if you're reading this book, it's because you want to increase your influence *everywhere*. Sure, there are places you'll have more pull than others, whether at work or home, with vendors, employees, or clients. One place many people go wrong is in limiting the range of contexts in which they even think about being influential. They think, "Well, in this big meeting I want to have more influence." Or they think only short-term specifics, like wanting to do a good job on an upcoming presentation. When going in for your annual review, for example, you'd certainly hope to have some positive influence in the outcome since there's a good chance your raise, bonus, or promotion opportunity will be discussed. But this kind of thinking is missing the forest for the trees.

Influence is most likely to happen when people enter a conversation ready to receive information from you that they anticipate will be useful. When they expect to hear interesting, valuable ideas and give you the benefit of the doubt that you will deliver, that's when they are most open to your powers of persuasion.

If you go to speak with someone and your reputation is as a person who exudes executive presence—poised, thoughtful, and insightful, with consistently valuable ideas to contribute—when you walk through their door, the person you are meeting will be expecting the same quality experience. They anticipate quality that will be worth their time and attention.

On the other hand, if you have the reputation of someone who is myopic, scattered, overly aggressive, or undiplomatic (or, alternatively, a bit meek, hesitant, or otherwise not confident), people will brace themselves in anticipation of what you will (or won't) say. They'll be wondering what they have to do in order to have a productive conversation, much less make it a pleasant experience. At that point, you're behind the eight-ball with expectations to *undo* before you can reset and get anyone to hear the true value of what you're saying. This undermines your effectiveness and your results.

You have to learn to use all of the skills, strategies, and tactics we've been discussing in *every* conversation you have. Whether you're on stage in front of five thousand people or sitting in the back of the conference room with a dozen other people, listening to someone else present, where your only participation might be asking a question at the end, it all still applies toward establishing your reputation and influence potential.

I always tell my clients to remember one simple but powerful rule of thumb: *Your reputation is what happens in the moments when you are not trying.* In crunch time, yes, it's good if you 'get your act together' and come through at the eleventh hour, and represent yourself, your case, or the company well, but it shouldn't have to take that kind of eleventh hour pressure for you to step up. Your reputation starts with *who others know you to be*. What you *can* do when you really *have to* is secondary.

**Your reputation is what happens in
the moments when you are not trying.**

It's the conversations at the coffee pot, in run-of-the-mill Monday morning team meetings, or standing by the elevator that people see you at your "default" setting. Daily check-in conversations with a client, heart-to-hearts with an underperforming employee, and casual conversations in the cafeteria all contribute to what kind of person others believe you to be at your core. That's where they see who you *really* are, deep down, rather than who you *try* to be when you think someone important is looking. Trust me, people see and remember both images of you, and are crystal-clear in their understanding of the difference.

The question you have to ask yourself is: "How do I show up during all those other times?"

It's not that you should act "presidential" every moment of the day with some stiff, overly-regal sort of façade. But ask yourself, for example: "In my conversations, do I regularly use up-speak?" For that matter, do you even know if you do? Most people who habitually do it are usually unaware of their habit (as I mentioned in Chapter 4) because it is set solidly in their blind spot.

Of course, it's not just vocal delivery that matters. Consider your *visual messaging*. Are you a constant fidgeter, touching your hair and face, or jamming your hands in your pockets? Do you dress in clothes that are revealing, or a notch or two below or above industry standards of professional formality? For example, if you're on a movie production crew, it's expected that you'll dress in a tee-shirt and shorts, so coming to work in a three-piece suit is every bit as out of place as a banker entering a meeting with the board of directors wearing a tee-shirt, jeans, and flip-flops.

What about your *verbal channel*? Do you tell jokes inappropriate for the workplace? (For example, if I were speaking at a PETA [People for the Ethical Treatment of Animals] event, I would never tell the grasshopper story I used in Chapter 3.) Do you drop a "four-letter word" here and there? Do you constantly use fillers? Do you have a hard time getting to the point with your stories and explanations? These are all behaviors that can contribute to how *others* would define your executive presence, and this is directly related to the influence they believe you can and will have in any given situation.

If you do any of these habitually, what are the odds that your supervisors in the corner office will give you the opportunity to prove that you *are* the person who can lead the big sales meeting with the new multi-million-dollar client? Can they trust that at crunch time, you'll suddenly be able to break those habits? My guess is that it is unlikely at best because your reputation precedes you, even if you *could* technically "turn it off." It's not worth the risk for them if they have repeatedly seen your standard manner, regardless of what you *claim* is possible.

That's not to say that you can't let your hair down when having lunch with a coworker, but when you do, how *much* do you let it down? At that point, how does it influence their perception of you, much less what they tell others?

Ultimately, you have to proactively identify and close that blind spot, making positive new practices and habits your new normal. Constant mindfulness and vigilance are critical in order to make sure they become your new reputation.

So, what are some of the contexts in which we need to start being more mindful of our leadership communication and influence? Let's look at a few of the big ones. But let me clarify: These next sections are not about "Public Speaking 101" or an introduction to presentation skills. We're going to focus here on shifting the whole approach to speaking in these contexts and others to ensure that you maximize your powers of positive influence.

## II.  PUBLIC SPEAKING

First, let's get one thing straight. When most people think about "public speaking" events, they assume immediately it's about being on stage at a conference or similar event, probably standing at a podium with a microphone and a big screen behind them. This is incorrect.

*Public speaking is what you are doing any time you are speaking to someone other than yourself.* Are you on a conference call? You're public speaking. Having a networking conversation with someone over coffee or lunch? You're public speaking. An impromptu meeting with an employee? You're public speaking. And yes, if you're on stage in that formal podium-microphone-spotlight kind of environment, that's public speaking too. But regardless of venue or audience size, in each of these contexts, you need to apply everything we've been discussing about speech alignment and credibility if you want to reinforce your leadership image and reputation.

That formal on-stage context is the one comedian Jerry Seinfeld was most likely referring to when he observed that if, according to a study, the average person's top fear was speaking in front of a crowd and the second biggest fear was death, then at any given funeral more people would rather be in the coffin than delivering the eulogy. What is it about the concept of "public speaking" that makes people want to run for the hills?

## A.  Fear of Public Speaking

Actually, at the heart of the fear of public speaking is not the notion of speaking in public, *per se*. In reality, it's the fear of public *scrutiny* or public *judgment*. Most people are terrified that they'll make a mistake or forget what they were supposed to say and look foolish in front of everyone. There's an irrational and mean little voice in the back of their minds that says, "Don't screw up, or you'll never be respected again!"

I have coached every kind of professional imaginable on leadership communication, and the most common excuse I hear (note that I said *excuse*, not *reason*) for people's lack of skill or confidence in their public speaking skills is the modern "get out of jail free" card: "I'm not good at public speaking because I'm an introvert."

Whether for contexts as mundane as weekly departmental meetings or as exciting as giving a TED talk, this refrain is as erroneous as it is self-destructive and, frankly, it's tiresome. That's why I want to take a moment to do some myth-busting about introverts and public speaking. I'll share a few strategies so that—whether you're an introvert or not—you can improve your skills and confidence when you have to speak in public.

## B.   Public Speaking and Myth-Busting

First, the myth-busting. There is a lot of confusion about what it actually means to be an introvert, *per se*. Introversion is what tools like the Myers-Briggs Type Indicator (MBTI) or DiSC assessment refer to as a *preference*, or natural inclination. By MBTI's parameters, for example, introversion pertains to what kinds of situations *give* you energy, and which *cost* you energy. If you feel more energized after leaving a party because of the fun "rush" you got, you're probably more extroverted; if you feel drained at the end of the party and need some "alone time" to recharge your batteries, *even if you had a blast,* you're probably more introverted.

Of course there are many other characteristics of introverts as well, but the problem is that most people mistakenly use the word *introvert* as a more intellectual-sounding synonym for "shy." Shy people inherently feel distress in certain public contexts. Introverts and extroverts alike can feel the same kind of anxiety when giving a formal presentation, which can stem from a variety of factors such as who the audience is and what is at stake.

Introverts, on the other hand, can be just as comfortable on stage as extroverts. I have numerous friends and colleagues who are self-proclaimed introverts who love to lead seminars and give presentations, but don't like networking events or parties with more than a few people present. For that matter, I know plenty of extroverts who claim to hate public speaking just as much as the introverts do. So, just because your Myers-Briggs classification or DiSC profile labeled you as an introvert, don't let it mislead you into believing that you are genetically programmed to hate or be bad at public speaking, and don't blame your current comfort level with public speaking on the classification. That excuse no longer works!

If you're someone who stresses out about public speaking, regardless of where you fall on the introvert-extrovert continuum, here are a few tips to help you feel confident and deliver your presentation with authority.

## 1.  The Four-Word Secret to Speaking with Confidence

First and foremost, you need a mindset shift. Most people feel nervous because they barrage themselves with a bunch of self-defeating, worst-case-scenario questions: "What if I make a mistake? What if I forget what I want to say? What if they don't like me? What if...."

Sound familiar?

Here's the short version of my advice: STOP. Stop yourself the minute you catch yourself starting down this path. That kind of negative self-talk will accomplish nothing other than to undermine your confidence. Why do that to yourself?

---

*Once I was talking to Elaine, a client whose inner critic was getting the best of her. I said: "I'm going to tell you a secret that will change everything. It's just four little words, but they're the secret to speaking with complete confidence. I want you to write them down in big letters, and tape the message to your computer, bathroom mirror, laptop, door, or anywhere you'll see it regularly. Will you do that?"*

*"Yes," she agreed, and grabbed her pen.*

*Then I told her the secret: "IT'S...NOT...ABOUT...YOU."*

*She wrote it down, then stared at it, digesting its meaning.*

*"Here's the key," I explained. "When you give any presentation, your focus should be on 'customer service.' Your primary responsibility and goal is to ensure that the audience has the best experience possible. Is your topic important for them? Is it interesting? Do you love it? Help them understand why, and share that passion with them."*

*"Don't be afraid to make eye contact," I told her. "Each and every person there wants to feel like you're talking to them personally. Like they're the only person there. Look at each person with that goal in mind, let them know that they matter to you. It makes them feel like they're part of the event, and that's critical."*

*I could see that she was processing what I was telling her. "Think about it," I said. "When you go to hear a speaker, do you sit there critiquing them, hoping to catch a mistake? Of course not.*

---

*If they make lots of mistakes or flounder, that makes everyone uncomfortable. You're just hoping they'll be interesting and give you some important information to make it worth your while to have shown up. You are rooting for their success, because if they do well, you'll have a good experience, which is what you really want in the end. That's exactly what your audience is hoping for from you too."*

*Elaine was quiet for a moment.*

*"How do you feel about that?" I asked.*

*"Honestly?" she said, "As soon as you said it's not about me, I instantly felt relieved. I can focus on taking care of the audience, because it is important that they feel like they learned something important. Then it's not about being perfect, whatever that means. Suddenly, it all seems like a very reachable goal. I know I can do this."*

## 2. Be the Speaker You'd Want to Hear

Once you stop looking at the opportunity from an ego-driven perspective (e.g. "How do I look good?") and start looking at it from a generosity-driven perspective (e.g. "How can I give my audience the most valuable experience possible?"), ask yourself: "If I were in the audience, what information would I want to hear? What kind of delivery style or personality would I hope the speaker would demonstrate so I could connect with them and so they could hold my attention?" Once you've answered those questions, *be that speaker.*

*Mindset shift: Achieved.*

## C. The Sixty-to-Sixty Rule

Second, even if you don't have time to rehearse your whole presentation, *rehearse the first minute.* Not just once. Use your video camera on your phone and record yourself talking through your introduction so you can see where you're fumbling for words or are otherwise out of alignment, then decide how you would prefer to start. Re-record until you're happy with it— even if it's not perfect.

Why?

I call it the "Sixty-to-Sixty Rule." That means that in *the first sixty seconds* of speaking, you will set people's expectations for the value you are going to contribute to *the next sixty minutes* of your time together. That first minute is your on-ramp to the highway of your talk. If you're like most people, you start to feel more comfortable and confident once you get going and have gotten into your groove. The on-ramp, however, is bumpy because, ironically, you don't think you need to prepare the introduction because it's, well, "just the intro."

**The Sixty-to-Sixty Rule:**
**In the first sixty seconds of speaking,**
**you will set people's expectations**
**for the value you are going to contribute**
**to the next sixty minutes of your time together.**

"How hard is it to welcome everyone and get started?" is a common rhetorical question. Simply put, the answer is: "Harder than you think." In theory, yes, the concept is simple, but thinking back to your *alignment diagram*, remember that your *verbal, vocal, and visual channels* need to be in sync in order for you to sound comfortable, focused, and authentic. More often than not, you'll realize that it will take at *least* two or three run-throughs before you successfully welcome everyone in a way that satisfies you and sets the right tone for the rest of the event.

Plus, getting your introduction right has a *huge* effect on your confidence. When you aren't grinding along uncomfortably in first gear—because you know exactly what you want to say from the moment you open your mouth—it eliminates the jitters and allows you to hit the ground running, exuding genuine confidence from the start.

In addition, remember that being *relatable* is more important than being *perfect*. Regardless of your relative status, talk to the audience as peers:

- share anecdotes,
- tell a well-timed joke if you think it's appropriate and you can nail the punch line (do *not* attempt a joke if you are not naturally a funny person),
- laugh at yourself if you misspeak in a harmless way,

- if you're sharing good news, *smile* when you say it so you confirm that it is indeed good news, and
- invite questions and comments from the audience, time permitting. If you can't answer one, thank the person for the question, acknowledge that you don't have the information on hand but that when the meeting is over you'll find and share it.

*Relatability* is also where your storytelling skills come into play. When you tell a good story, and tell it well, people forget themselves and get lost in the flow, in the best way possible. This is one of the best ways to defeat what I call "the smart-phone factor." You see, your greatest competition in capturing and maintaining your audience's attention is a little three-by-six-inch device in each person's pocket or bag (or, more likely—hand), that sings an unrelenting siren song, wooing its owner with promises of something—anything—that will be so much more interesting than whatever you're talking about. Email, text messages, Facebook updates, Tweets, stock reports, sports scores...the list goes on and on.

So, how can you command the audience's attention and sustain it, beating the smart-phone factor? You have to be *relatable*.

Each of these strategies is crucial to commanding the room, whether it's at a conference podium or on a conference call. For those of you who truly *are* introverts, take all the alone-time you need to think through your introduction and presentation before you deliver it, and take some time after it's done in order to reflect and recharge. For that matter, if you're an extrovert, it's a good idea to do this too. And whether you're an introvert *or* an extrovert, it's always a good idea to debrief with someone else after it's over and compare notes on how it went. Constructive feedback, whether positive or negative, is critical to your continuing growth and your increasing powers of influence.

## III. PRESENTATIONS

One of the most commonly experienced kinds of "public speaking" is the official "presentation." Every time you turn around, someone is giving another presentation, whether it's as a student in class, a sales rep in front of a client, an entrepreneur pitching to investors, or an executive at a board meeting. Every presentation has *so much potential* to be interesting and inspiring, but they are all-too-frequently disappointing. Often, people set "good enough" as the bar they have to hurdle, but there is no valid excuse for allowing "good enough" to be your trademark standard for presenting.

Again, "good enough" generally implies that you have met the minimum standard of providing the necessary information. You've touched upon the basic "what," the verbal core of your message, but you have all but completely ignored the vocal and visual "how" in your delivery. And, more often than not, the "what" isn't even that compelling. It's just facts and figures, the spoken equivalent of a spreadsheet. Yawn. Hardly inspirational.

## A.   Train Your Inner Jockey

Remember, investors have an expression: *Bet the jockey, not the horse.* In other words, no matter how good the business "horse" might appear, it's the confidence the investors have in the person leading it that will ultimately make or break their decision to get on board and commit to riding it together. Even if it's not your company, it's still your product, service, or idea that you're pitching to your audience. If you want their buy-in, "good enough" simply isn't...well...good enough.

A common mistake presenters make is being too shallow in the value of their contribution, regardless of the amount of detail they include. Often, the tendency is merely to walk the audience through the work, bullet by bullet, row by row, or column by column, reading the data aloud off the slide or handout. The problem is that an audience can read the data for themselves—faster than the presenter can read it aloud. At that point, the person presenting isn't adding any value beyond a soundtrack, and it would have been far more efficient if they had simply emailed the files to everyone to read at their own convenience.

If you present in this way, you have missed the bigger purpose. You are lost in the weeds again. Your audience wants you to do an analysis, a deeper application, or an extrapolation. At this stage, you are more intimately familiar with the data than anyone, and often they want you to give a recommendation or share an insight that isn't obvious from the numbers themselves. This is your opportunity to shine, to persuade, to have influence. Remember that your audience wants you to answer one very important question: "So what?"

Realize that your ability to influence is 100 percent controlled by whether or not you have come up with a unique idea that you believe is important enough to share. Your data may show important information, and the audience may come up with their own conclusions after reading it, but at that point it's your *data* that is influential...*not you.* Could you let your work speak for itself? Sure, you could. But *don't.*

For example, instead of just telling your audience what the total revenue is in cell D49 of your spreadsheet, tell them what it means. Why is it significant? Of all the numbers there, why did cell D49's figure attract your attention? Why should it impact their decision? What are the causes, and what does that imply moving forward? Do we want to try to achieve this number again or not? Is the number repeatable if we want it to be, or preventable if we don't? How?

For a while I was working with Pete, the CFO of an insurance company. Pete's leadership ambitions were to rise to the CFO position in the parent company, but he lacked gravitas, the presence that makes people sit up and take notice. Pete would sit in quarterly finance meetings and other monthly meetings, and for each one he was expected to lead part of the discussion. Except that there was no discussion.

When it came to his part, Pete would hand out spiral-bound reports—maybe twenty to thirty pages long—to each person. Although there was a table of contents, it was basically twenty to thirty pages of spreadsheets. Row upon row and column after column of numbers, Pete would methodically walk everyone through those numbers section by section, virtually a human soundtrack, narrating each cell's contents. The problem with this—aside from it being painfully boring to listen to—was that Pete's presence added absolutely nothing of value to the meeting, so it was inefficient on top of boring!

## B.  Speaking Strategically

So, what was the cause of Pete's problem, and how did we solve it? First, he had to get clear on the difference between reciting the data and *telling the story* of the data, and how the latter changes people's entire perspective about it. Just like Pete, when you are presenting, it's your chance to provide additional information and unique insights that someone could *not* figure out for themselves upon merely reading or hearing the data. While the audience *might* have the skills and knowledge needed to read and understand the data in general, *you* are the one who spent all the time collating, culling, and analyzing it, so you should have unique insights to share that they don't have time to deduce, even if they could.

Those insights could include examples of how a situation was handled with certain clients or contracts, if any unique outlier skewed the results, how that should be prevented in the future, or a recommendation for moving forward and what that path might look like.

In his case, Pete realized that he had been so focused on the numbers, he had never stepped back to think about how to be more strategic in his approach to those meetings: both strategic in his approach to running them and what he shared, and strategic with regard to sharing his vision for what the numbers revealed and the direction he believed the company should take as a result. Once he was able to share his most important insights by looking at the greater forest, rather than the individual trees, the energy of the meetings changed, and so did his reputation and opportunity for advancement.

Meetings are an opportunity not just to share data, but to project into the future what it will all mean, drawing participants' attention to a specific cell, bullet, or image, revealing why it is of note, what's not obvious, and why they need to acknowledge it and work with it in the future. This is showing them your vision. This is how you get recognized for being more interesting AND more valuable. It's how you get noticed and appreciated.

## C.    PowerPoint: A Double-Edged Sword

While we're on the subject of meetings, of all the business and productivity tools out there, I truly believe that the greatest mixed blessing is PowerPoint (or Keynote if you are exclusively a Mac user.) Corporate America decries "death by PowerPoint," at least in theory, and yet more often than not promotes it vigilantly. If you want to be a captivating and influential presenter and plan to use slides in one form or another, there are several commandments that *thou shalt not forsake*, i.e., that are absolutely required. Nevertheless, there are also some well-intentioned but horribly misguided company practices that fly in the face of those guidelines.

### 1.   When is a Presentation not a Presentation?

First and foremost, it's crucial to distinguish between a report and a presentation. A *report* is a written document that is intended to be read, regardless of what kind of software is used to create the document, such as Microsoft Word, Excel, or PowerPoint. A *presentation* is delivered orally; the key information is narrated by a presenter, frequently using visual aids such as PowerPoint slides, which can be projected on a screen for everyone to view together. A "deck" is the business term used to reference a set of slides used. Unfortunately, in many organizations, the deck that is projected in the front of the room is the exact same deck that is printed out and used as handouts in the same meeting. Why is this a problem?

Years ago, early in my consulting career, I did work for an organization which had a mandate from the top that said that presentation slides must be so comprehensively clear that they could be standalone documents. To me, that was a disaster waiting to happen, because it renders the presenter obsolete!

If that's the case, you don't need to be there, so why hold a meeting? Send the file to everyone by email, have them read it, and convene at some other point to discuss—but don't waste everybody's time getting together for a meeting, just so people can read the same file at the same time.

Unsurprisingly, those rules were created by someone who had no intention of being at the meeting, but wanted to be able to skim the deck and know what it is about. Perhaps their edict was insurance so that if a key stakeholder, such as an investor or the board, wanted to check up on something, then they could see it and have all their questions answered independently. That's a logical concern in general, but it prioritizes the needs and the desires of the few (who will *not* be present) over the needs of all those who *will* be sitting in the meeting (dying a death by a thousand mental paper cuts in the process).

Just because you choose to write up your information in PowerPoint rather than in traditional word processing software doesn't mean you've created a presentation. For example, ask yourself: "Did I use ten- or twelve-point font (or even smaller) in order to fit everything on the page?" If so, accept that it is still a report. Ideally, presentations should not use anything smaller than twenty-point font.

At best, if you still need to have a comprehensive deck for someone to read offline (perhaps, say, as pre-reading material for the board before the annual meeting), then you should *have a second version* of the deck which is intended to maximize the learning experience of the attendees at the meeting in which it is presented.

## 2.    Your Relationship with Your Slides

How do you maximize that experience, you may ask? You need to understand the relationship between the presenter and the deck. To explain by way of a musical analogy, there is no "Sonny and Cher" relationship between presenter and deck. Sonny and Cher were a duo in the '60s and '70s who shared the stage. Sometimes Sonny led, sometimes Cher did, but they were equal partners from start to finish. When it comes to your professional presentation, however, there is no fifty-fifty, where the audience will spend half the time looking at the slides and half the time listening to you.

Instead, there's only a Motown-esque "Gladys Knight and the Pips" kind of relationship, where one of the two of you (you or your slides) is the star. Like Gladys Knight, you want to have the majority of the audience's attention focused on you as the star, the center of attention, and the primary conveyor of information. The PowerPoint deck should be relegated to the role of a "Pip," a backup singer who adds context, harmony, some visual details but is not—and never will be—the star of the show. Following this guideline will be "The Best Thing That Ever Happened..." to you *and* your audience.

The moral of this story should be: If you are a presenter, don't be a Pip. How do you do that? A simple rule of thumb is to never put more information on a slide and up on the screen than you are talking about at that moment. You want to be the focus, the attention, the center, the persuader, the source. The goal is for the audience to glance at the new information on the screen, easily get the gist, and then immediately turn their attention back to you to contextualize, extrapolate, and make it interesting and relevant.

### a.   *The 5x5 Rule*

For example, say your first slide has three bullet points. For starters, simplify the wording as much as possible. A commonly referenced guideline is the "five-by-five" rule, where no slide can have more than five bullets, with a maximum of five words per bullet. Can you have three bullets with eight words or vice versa? Sure, but it's not so much about the math as the intention of minimizing the amount of reading comprehension required and visual clutter on each slide. As long as the text clearly identifies the topic, *you* can vocalize the rest of what would have been up there. Let the audience rely on *you* for the explanation, not on the screen.

"But wait," you might protest, "My company's rule is to keep it to as few slides as possible. Isn't that a good idea?" In theory, yes. But if the result is just creating a minimum number of slides that are all maximally painful to sit through, you've missed the point.

Imagine that your teenager comes home and says, "Mom, Dad, I absolutely *neeeed* these new basketball sneakers."

"How much?" you ask.

"Two hundred dollars."

"Two hundred dollars?! *My* shoes don't even cost that much."

"Yeah, but it's actually not all that much," your teen explains. "You only need to give me *two bills!*"

Of course, whether it's two one-hundred-dollar bills or two hundred singles, it's still the same amount of money. Similarly, when you have an hour's worth of material, whether you cram it all onto two slides that take you thirty minutes apiece to painstakingly (and painfully) decipher, or spread it out among sixty simple slides that you can move through quickly, it's still the same amount of material. The only (massive) difference is in the audience's experience.

### b.   *Visual Focal Point*

But even if you can't do this with all of your slides (in a situation where, for example, you have figures, a big table, or complex diagrams to show), you still need to help the audience know where to look and when, to be able to follow your train of thought. The challenge is that the audience's eyes and ears are in competition with each other. They can work together if they're both seeing and hearing the same thing, but if the ears are hearing something that is markedly different from what the eyes are looking at, the eyes *always* win.

This is because with sound, as soon as a word is uttered—*poof*—it's gone. If the listener didn't catch something in the moment it was said, too bad, they missed it. But they *can* trust the permanence of the text, relying on their ability to go back and read it as often as they want until they've wrapped their head around it, and then move on.

The worst part is that when they need to work to understand what they read because your slide looks like the front page of the New York Times, you are no longer either Gladys Knight *or* a Pip because all they hear is an instrumental "Wawaah, wahwaah waaaaah…." which they are tuning out, and they have turned off your microphone.

So, whether you have bullets, tables, diagrams, images, or something else, the key is to reveal only as much information as you're going to discuss at any moment. Whether you animate your slides so that each bullet pops up when you're ready to go over it, or a red arrow moves around a table or chart with your talk so the audience always knows which cell you're addressing, or you gray-out parts of a diagram that you don't want distracting the audience when you're talking about another part, you can ensure that you are the star and the audience is with you every step of the way.

When in doubt, remember the moral of the story: Don't be a Pip!

## IV. SENSITIVE CONVERSATIONS

One context that is difficult for many people, and can be even more stress-inducing than public speaking engagements, is what I call "thin ice" conversations. These are the topics where you know that you are discussing a particularly sensitive issue, and with one false move, tempers can flare, defensiveness can rise, egos can get bruised, or people can shut down or attack…and if any of those things happen, whatever goal you had in mind for that conversation goes right out the window. It's like ice skating on a frozen lake, and hearing the ice start to crackle, a warning that it's precariously thin. You have to navigate carefully, watching where you go and how you maneuver…if you take one wrong step, the ice could crack and you'll plunge right through.

## A.  Diplomacy

Diplomacy is one of the most delicate and nuanced skill sets you'll ever develop. There are some clever quotations about it, such as "Diplomacy is the art of letting someone have your way" (Daniele Varè), or "Tact (Diplomacy) is the ability to tell someone to go to hell in such a way that they look forward to the trip" (Winston Churchill).

Joking aside, the ability to balance clarity of meaning with diplomacy in a way that is maximally productive while maintaining and even *strengthening* the relationships among the people involved is both a science and an art that we all could spend a lifetime trying to master.

When you know you have to have a conversation with someone about a topic that might not make them happy, the goal is to conduct the conversation in a way that will help keep emotions at bay and allow sincerity, transparency, and honesty to lead the way while preserving people's feelings, allowing them to save face, and seeking solutions either to rectify the situation or compensate for it.

Unfortunately, it's common for people to go to one extreme or the other. If you are particularly conflict-averse, for example, you might habitually try to avoid those confrontations by dodging the people and the subject, hoping that the problem will resolve itself eventually. On the other hand, you might prefer to run in headlong, believing that the easiest thing to do is to rip the Band-Aid off, so you blurt out the first words that come to mind. At that point, you've been clear, but most likely in a way that ended up being hurtful, and that will inevitably escalate from simple conflict into combat...which is neither desirable nor necessary.

## B.  Diplomacy and Goal-Setting

In these situations, it is critical to have a clear vision of your ideal outcome for a conversation, understanding which qualities need to shine through most brightly to achieve this outcome. Do you need to project determination? Concern? Something else? Then you have to really think about your alignment: what you will say, how you want your message to land, and how you are going to deliver it to get that desired outcome. All of this requires strategic planning to maximize the likelihood of both achieving the outcome you desire *and* maintaining the integrity of the relationship, as opposed to haphazardly tossing a veritable grenade on the whole situation.

When my husband Larry and I were first married, we would get into the occasional argument about something or other, and sometimes when he ran out of patience with the issue, feeling like it hadn't come to a resolution quickly enough, he would shift gears and pull out what was then his "trump card" response. A lawyer by education and profession, he would state firmly, "Look, I was trained in logic...," as primary evidence for why his perspective was the correct one on the subject.

Now, this might be what he was thinking at the time. And I'm sure that in that moment, in his mind, his argument was perfectly logical. However, whenever he used this line on me, what I heard was: "Twenty-five years ago, I went to graduate school for three years and took a class in logic, while I don't believe your ten years of graduate school provided you any such skill set, so as a result I must always be right, you must always be wrong, and you need to accept it."

Needless to say, this didn't land well. The first couple of times he said it, I took the bait, got defensive, and it turned into a volley of fruitless arguing. The third time he used it, I caught myself. I knew I didn't want a repeat of the previous experience, so I stopped in my tracks, collected myself, stepped out of the conversation content-wise, and said, "Hon, when you make that statement I can't continue the conversation with you anymore. Because what you are claiming is that your three years of law school from twenty-five years ago made you a master of logic. For you, that's the only thing that matters because that's where you were first taught logic, whereas my ten years of Master's and PhD work taught me nothing but illogic and nonsense, so I should just accept that anytime we disagree I must be wrong because you're smart and I'm not. And I find that to be not only inaccurate, but insulting. Can you understand how that statement makes it impossible for me to continue to work through this issue with you?"

What was most important was that I was in alignment when I said it:

- First, my words were carefully selected and objective, with no insults, subjective interpretations, or name-calling,
- Second, my body language was deliberately neutral, and

■ Third, my voice was calm and controlled but still clear and unwavering. I simply laid out the facts of his statement and how I perceived their meaning, and asked him if he could see the connection between the two. I was neither attacking him nor being defensive.

To Larry's credit, he also was able to step back and be objective, recognizing how I could interpret his message as I had done. He clarified that he did indeed have full respect for my academic credentials, communication skills as a professional, and overall intelligence as a person. Most importantly, he committed to me that he would never revert to using that response again. Thankfully, he has kept his promise and our occasional disagreements stay more balanced and productive.

As I discovered, when you are looking to avoid escalating a conversation into full crisis-mode, or to redirect it and bring it down a few notches if it has already reached that level, you absolutely have to think about what kind of outcome you want to have. Then you need to think about how you are going to get there. Consider what you should and should not say based on how you believe others are likely to respond to certain content and ideas. Then make sure that you are mindful and in control of your delivery so that they hear not just your content, but your sincere *intent* behind it.

I was able to control my body language, control my words, and control my tone of voice, keeping it all calm and neutral (even though I was not smiling or happy), which allowed us to redirect the conversation. We detached ourselves from the emotion and frustration in the topic, and took a step back, so when we resumed the discussion, we were both able to start over with clear heads and a shared mutual purpose: coming to a common understanding for the issue at hand while speaking to each other with loving respect, and setting a new path for future disagreements as well.

It's no different whether you are talking to a fifth-grader or a fifty-year-old (whether student, spouse, or CEO). All people want the same things: To feel respected, and to know that they have been heard...even if they can't ultimately get their way.

# V. MEETINGS

Possibly the most frequently *missed* opportunity to demonstrate leadership and have a strong, positive influence is in the regular, mundane occurrence of meetings. This includes the meetings that we look forward to; the meetings we dread; the routine, humdrum, status update meetings; the exciting prospective client meetings; and everything in between.

What tends to happen is that people default to their most instinctive behavior in meetings, because they want the meeting to end as quickly as possible, they want to push certain subjects until they get their way, or they want to avoid particular subjects so as not to be vulnerable. What that translates to is that there are usually a few people who do most of the talking, a few people who occasionally chime in, and a few people who prefer to stay in the background, only speaking when addressed personally, or if their contribution on a specific issue has been planned ahead of time. The problem is that everyone should be taking on all three of these roles at different times. It is important to understand when it is appropriate to assume each role, so ask yourself:

- "When should I dig assertively for more information?
- When should I speak up and interject with an important observation or question?
- Alternatively, when should I sit back and just listen for the sole purpose of understanding everything that is going on, to recognize other people's perspectives, with the intention of digesting all the information and coming back at a later time with some possible solutions?"

Most of us, however, tend to stick with whichever of these tendencies are in our comfort zone, and this allows myriad opportunities to demonstrate leadership simply to pass us by.

If you are the facilitator, it's not just your job to walk everyone through the list of items on the agenda. In this case, ask yourself:

- "Do I try to referee the interactions to ensure that one or two people don't dominate inappropriately?

> ※ Do I seek input from those who might otherwise not voluntarily come forth with their perspectives, no matter how valuable those perspectives might be?
>
> ※ Do I welcome respectful contradiction and challenges at the conference table, or do I do my best to shoot down anyone who disagrees with me? Can I discuss these disagreements and challenges objectively, respectfully, and diplomatically, or do I feel like any disagreement is a personal attack and threat to my reputation and possibly even my job security?"

What does confidence look like in this context, and how does the way you navigate it impact your reputation?

What about if you are not facilitating the meeting, but it's your turn to share an update? I'm always surprised at how many people only direct an answer to the person at the head of the room, instead of looking at everyone there. It's important to engage everyone to indicate that they matter to you as much as the person running the show.

When participation dynamics are imbalanced or worse, the overall value of the meeting suffers for everyone.

A few years ago, I was doing some consulting work for a bank, and sat in on one of the oddest—and worst—meetings I'd ever attended. The room was enormous, with one ridiculously long, skinny conference table along the side. There were around twenty people sitting on each side of the table and—God help them—there was a conference phone in the middle. The convener, Bruce, and his inner circle were down towards one end of the table, and all the analysts were at the other end. I can't imagine who the poor soul sitting at the other end of the conference call was.

When the meeting got going, Bruce's group did most of the talking among themselves, audibly enough so that everyone could hear. Every now and then they'd ask an analyst to share some data, at which point they would all look at their spreadsheet printouts, and someone at the far end of the table would mumble a few points in such a soft voice that no one but those seated close by could hear anything they said.

What shocked me most was that *not one person asked the mumblers to speak up.* Everyone just spent the time reading the spreadsheet for themselves until the droning ended. What a huge waste of time and opportunity!

Afterward, I met with Sam, one of the analysts (and mumblers) at that meeting. I asked about the meeting and he confirmed that it was the usual flow. I shared with him, "I was sitting about ten feet away from you, and couldn't hear what you said. I can't imagine Bruce did either. I know you have a naturally gentle voice, but when you speak so softly, the message you ultimately send is that you don't have confidence in your work so you don't believe it's important that everyone else hears what you have to say. And worse than that, the fact that nobody asked you to speak more loudly indicated that they agreed: They didn't think your comments were important enough to listen to!"

The next week I met with Andrew, another client who was also in those meetings. He smiled, and opened with, "Did you hear about this week's meeting?"

"No," I replied, curious. "What happened?"

"When it was Sam's turn to share the update, he pushed his chair back and stood up, then spoke loudly—for him—so everyone could hear. I was sitting down by Bruce, who raised his eyebrows, leaned over to me and said, 'What got into him?'"

When I saw Sam later that day, I asked him how the meeting went. He confirmed he had changed his delivery, and when I asked why, he said, "I worked really hard on those reports! It was important and I wanted everyone to know it." That day, his reputation and career outlook took a turn for the better.

Those are the moments that give others the incentive to offer you the leadership role more often. Don't pass up those seemingly run-of-the-mill opportunities to demonstrate the leader that you truly are...and the leader you want to be.

# VI.  ONE-ON-ONE CONVERSATIONS

## A.  Priorities in Context

Context is everything, especially in one-on-one conversations. For example, as noted earlier, Toastmasters is an internationally renowned organization that helps people master the art of public speaking. It's a great organization and I've referred many people there for a variety of reasons. The skills they teach are widely applicable, but they need to be applied differently in each context to be effective. After all, the term "toast-master" was first assigned to a person who gave the toast, or the speech at an event. The problem is that most people who interact with you do *not* want you to launch into a full-blown speech!

*I once had to "undo" a bit of the speech habits that a client, Pam, had developed at Toastmasters. She had excelled there, was poised and organized in her speaking, and never used fillers; the word "um" was not part of her vocabulary. Yet she came to me because, in spite of her training, she had a reputation of being rather cold, unapproachable, and lacking in emotional intelligence.*

*Now there are certainly plenty of leaders out there who could stand to brush up on these areas themselves, but they were particularly important for Pam because she was in human resources.*

*Think about it: Why do people go to speak with their HR representative? It's typically because they have a problem and need a solution. They have a question about benefits after an unplanned hospital stay, or they want to get reimbursed for something, or maybe they want to report hostile working conditions.*

*Whatever the reason, they don't go to HR for fun, so when they are presenting these personal, embarrassing, or face-threatening challenges, the last thing they care about is whether or not you let an "um" or two slip out. They do not want to know that you can recite policy smoothly, or that you are poised and graceful in your movements.*

*They want to be understood. They want compassion and empathy. They want reassurance that you will help them resolve their issue. They are looking for comfort and security.*

*But this was not what Pam was prioritizing or projecting. She wanted to be seen as polished; they wanted reassurance that she could relate. She had mastered the first C: Command the room, but at the expense of the second C: she failed to Connect with the audience. As a result, she was rarely able to achieve the third C and Close the deal, or establish her desired image and reputation as a leader who excelled in technical skill AND empathy, in these meetings.*

If you're in your office conducting your employee's annual review meeting, sincerity, authenticity, and integrity are crucial. That's a prerequisite to getting through all the necessary items on the agenda with mutual respect, and in a way that gets the critical points across unambiguously while still preserving and strengthening your relationship. You can give constructive feedback freely (and the employee will receive it freely) when your message is conveyed diplomatically, and you sound and look like you mean what you say. Alignment in your speech (and theirs) is crucial for this to be a productive, successful exchange, and for you to come across as a true leader.

## B.    Networking and Mindset

It's the same in networking, which is a public speaking event of its own. In Chapter 5: Visual, I told you about Chad, the financial advisor I had met for coffee who never made eye contact with me the entire time we were at the café. He might have known a lot about insurance and planning, but I was more interested in whether he was mentally present in our conversation. Based on his lack of alignment, I was convinced he was not.

Larger business networking events, interestingly, are polarizing in that people tend to either love them or hate them. Those who love them tend to enjoy the social aspect, and know how to use the experience to their benefit, extending their reach and expanding their business opportunities. In contrast, those who hate them often claim to be uncomfortable talking about themselves or otherwise don't know how to get value out of the experience beyond collecting a handful of random business cards. For both of those problems (much like I mentioned previously about getting over the fear of public speaking in general), the solution starts with a mindset shift.

### 1.    Love What You Do and Show It

First, if you enter an event thinking, "But I'm in accounting; people are going to think it's boring," or "I don't like to talk about myself," what you will project from the first handshake is a lack of confidence in who you are and what you do. At that point, regardless of what you say, the impression you make will be forgettable at best, or lasting and negative at worst.

A case in point is my relationship with my accountant. One of the things I love about my accountant is that he genuinely loves tax accounting. He's fascinated by the rules and loves to tell me about new ideas he has. Personally, I can't think of any job I would enjoy less than tax accounting, which is exactly why I stick with my guy. If I met an accountant who thought their own career was as boring as I thought their work was, I would never hire them. That's the kind of person who lacks commitment, attention to detail, and pride in their work. I want to work with a person who is passionate about offering the services I need, regardless of whether or not I think the subject area is interesting. If it's clear that *they* think their work is interesting, and *why* they like it, then I find *them* interesting. If they're in alignment when telling me about what they do, instinctively, I'm more willing to bet on that jockey.

## 2. Long-Term Goal Orientation

Second, realize that networking is a marathon, not a sprint, because it's about planting seeds and cultivating new, long-term, and potentially fruitful relationships. It's not a transactional occurrence with the goal of getting someone to hire you or buy from you today. The people I meet at a networking event rarely become my clients but the people *they* introduce me to *do*.

Remember the Third C: *Close the Deal*. But in this context, the initial "deal" to close might just be getting another introduction, recommendation or resource, or chance to provide valuable information to someone else.

If you approach an event from the perspective of simply meeting interesting people and seeing how *you* can be of value to *them*—whether by sending them an article link, making an introduction, or perhaps giving some advice, now or a year from now—you become memorable in a whole new, positive way. Bob Burg and John David Mann's *The Go Giver* is a great resource to read for deeper insights into relationship development as the purpose in networking.

So, no matter how informal or brief a one-to-one encounter might be, recognize that the way you show up will have a direct effect on the impression you make and the impact you have.

# VII. VIRTUAL CONVERSATIONS

## A. Phone Calls

One of the most dreaded events on most people's calendars is the telephone call. It's like a meeting, but worse: you can't see each other, the sound quality for some people's connection is often poor, and you can bet money that at least a few people are "multitasking" during the call, which usually means checking email instead of paying attention.

### 1. Projecting Leadership when Speaking "Blindly"

As I mentioned in Chapter 5: Visual, one of the biggest mistakes you can make is to let down your guard regarding your body language, under the misguided belief that people can't see you. (Remember, people can hear what you look like!) Since there is no visual input on a phone call, all people have to go on is your vocal input to color their interpretation of your words.

When you think about your alignment, recall that your voice and your body are physically connected. Your posture and facial expressions will influence the way you sound when you speak, influencing how people interpret what you say. If these three channels are not in alignment, your credibility will suffer.

A client, Lois, had been lobbying for a promotion to the executive ranks, and knew that she needed to improve her executive presence so that she could prove herself ready for the new role. As an assignment, I had her video record short excerpts of herself talking on the telephone to different people. She didn't need to record what they said, so privacy wasn't an issue; this was strictly an opportunity to watch and listen to herself, observing her own behavioral alignment and what impression it made in this context.

Our next session was scheduled for a couple of weeks out to discuss the patterns that had emerged, but she contacted me within twenty-four hours. She had already done several recordings and was dismayed to realize that she sounded like two different people depending on whom she was talking to. When she was talking to her direct reports (the people on her team), she was confident, her voice was strong, and her points were decisive. She was still approachable, not overbearing, but firm and direct.

However, when she was on the phone with her supervisor, the senior vice-president, she said, "It was like listening to a child. There was perpetual up-speak, I heard tons of fillers, my face looked like I was either angry or on the verge of tears...I don't know who that person was!"

Lois was suddenly clear on why her promotion kept getting deferred, despite her technical qualifications for the job. Through this exercise, she understood that although she was saying verbally that she was ready for the job, vocally and visually she was contradicting herself. Her words said that she was a confident expert, ready to lead, but when talking to key decision-makers, her delivery projected that she was easily intimidated and unsure of herself. She understood that when it came to the decision related to the promotion, the delivery of her message was far more influential than its content.

She recognized a massive discrepancy between the leader that her direct reports saw, and the follower that her boss saw. Our job became to close that gap and ensure that her boss saw the same side of her that everyone else did, so that the leader was the default persona that everyone saw, regardless of their position. If she couldn't do this on the phone, how could she do it in person? She refocused her preparation for these calls and other meetings, and within a couple of months, the VP spot was hers.

## 2.    Energy

Many people tell me that on the telephone, it is hard to get animated. They feel like they are just going through the motions because they are alone at their desk with the door closed, nobody else in sight. It's not surprising, since you're confined to a chair, immobile, your torso up against your desk, constraining your movement. You need to set yourself free, physically and mentally.

That's why I encourage you to stand up and move around when you talk on the phone. When you do that, your blood gets pumping and you naturally move in a way that takes up more space and projects more energy. You gesture more and your face and body "participate" in the conversation. Plus, standing helps with your breath support and voice quality. You project an entirely different level of energy, and your passion and enthusiasm can come through easily and authentically.

## B.  Conference Calls

Conference calls, especially when a group of people are all in one room talking to other people or groups through a speaker phone in the middle of the table, are probably the context in which I see the greatest *lack* of leadership communication. Too frequently, people in the same room only talk loudly enough for each other to hear, and the unfortunate person stuck on the other end of the line (let's call him "Bob") only catches bits and pieces of the conversation (sometimes despite making repeated requests for others to speak up, before silently giving up). In my opinion, the most regrettable effect I could have on someone is to know that they *gave up* trying to be engaged because I wasn't enabling them to do so. It's hardly a way to build loyalty, trust, and dedication.

Ultimately there are four people who are individually and collectively at fault for allowing this type of conference-call dynamic to happen: The speaker, the remote call participant, the convener, and everyone else. Why? Because each of them should have taken this as an opportunity to demonstrate leadership and ensure a meeting that was of maximum value to everyone involved. Let's look at who they are, and how they could have had a positive influence on everyone's experience on the call.

### 1.  Speaker Responsibility

The person who is speaking in the moment is the first person responsible to demonstrate leadership. If you are speaking, it's your responsibility to proactively and occasionally check with the person on the other end of the line: "Bob, just checking, can you hear me?"

### 2.  Remote Participant Responsibility

The second person is Bob. Like him, if you are the one in the remote location on the other end of the group call, it is your responsibility to reiterate—possibly multiple times—that you cannot hear whomever is talking. If you don't speak up, how will they know? Don't be embarrassed to ask more than once. If anything, it's the other participants who should be embarrassed that they're failing to include you in the conversation. You're being responsible. You are trying to contribute, investing your time in the meeting, so *do* keep politely but unambiguously nudging them to do so until they get the hint. Alternatively, if

153

they don't ever seem to get the hint, talk to the facilitator afterwards and work on guidelines for future conference call meetings to ensure that everyone is receiving all the critical information. It's an opportunity to demonstrate leadership and ensure the success of future engagements.

### 3.  Convener Responsibility

The third person who is responsible for Bob's unintentional exclusion is the convener of the meeting. If you called the meeting, it's incumbent upon you to ensure proactively that Bob and everyone remotely located has access to the information being shared. If you aren't on a platform like GoToWebinar or Zoom so that everyone is looking at your screen, but instead have some people who are only looking at their own local copy, be sure to cue them verbally every time you advance the slide, or want them to look at a different part of the current one, to ensure that their eyes and ears are getting the same input.

It's also up to you to check in with Bob to make sure he's following successfully, in case he isn't taking the initiative to speak up and tell you when he's lost. If it turns out that he can't hear certain people on your end or on other extensions, move the conference phone closer to them or vice versa, have them speak more loudly, or otherwise have the person closest to the phone repeat what was said to ensure everyone is included.

Is this slightly inconvenient? Possibly. But which is more important, the convenience of some, or the inclusion of all? Hopefully that was a rhetorical question and the answer is obvious. If you don't make this effort, you can bet Bob will give up and start checking his email, and you'll be revisiting the issue in the future when mistakes are made because of details missed on the call. In this case, you actually *have* the official leadership role, but failed to live up to the responsibility.

### 4.  Everyone Else's Responsibility

The fourth "person" who is responsible for the success or failure of ensuring that everyone is included is everybody else sitting at the table. Just because you're not the one speaking, you're not the one having a hard time hearing, or you're not the one facilitating the meeting, that doesn't mean you shouldn't take it upon yourself to try to help someone else if you realize that Bob is not likely to hear what someone else is saying. Don't use the excuse that it's "not your place" to interrupt, or that if Bob couldn't hear it was his responsibility to advocate for himself. Go ahead and politely interrupt to check on Bob and make suggestions to amend the situation if necessary. This is not a power play on your part; it's an act of generosity, teamwork, and leadership, making the cohesion of the full team the priority.

Remember: Your reputation is what happens in the moments when you're *not* trying. So, in those moments, what reputation are you building for yourself (even by doing *nothing*)? What influence are you going to have as a result?

## C. Video Conferencing

The last virtual context I want to address is the video conference. Whether you use Zoom, Skype, WebEx, FaceTime, GoToWebinar, Google Hangouts or an internal video platform, for many people and businesses, video conferencing is replacing the telephone and in-person meetings in many cases. Personally, I do most of my private coaching through video conferencing since the majority of my clients are not local. When I'm setting up a conversation with a new connection, I request video conferencing instead of telephone. Why? I believe we can get to know each other better when we make eye contact, see each other's facial expressions, and more. This creates a positive and lasting first impression and deepens the relationship.

The challenge with video conferencing, however, is that it is not quite a phone call, and not quite like being together in person. As a result, we can lack awareness of what 'appropriate presence' looks like in this new medium. It feels like body language and visual communication doesn't matter as much because the other person can only see us from the shoulders up. But the fact is, even though the other party can't see your body, they can tell when you're fidgeting. There's a discomfort projected, because whatever your body is doing from the neck down, it's telegraphed through what is visible from the neck up, through head and neck movements, the direction of your gaze, and other facial expressions.

Even the way that you are dressed still matters when you are video conferencing. Since your audience will only see you from the shoulders up, it's a common misconception that what you wear doesn't matter. But the truth is that if I'm having an important meeting with a client, student, or coworker with whom I have a more formal relationship, then I want to make sure I'm wearing a blouse or blazer that reflects the nature of our meeting. I'm not going to meet with a prospect online while wearing a tee-shirt. Instead, I'll wear something with a collar, or a blazer, and appropriate makeup and accessories. I know that what they see on the video screen is what they will use to form their impression of me.

Now, there is a time and a place for everything, and there are times when you can dress down for such an occasion. It may even help you be more relatable, whether virtually or otherwise.

*A little while ago I received a frantic email from JoAnn, a CFO from a billion-dollar company, saying, "Tomorrow afternoon we're having an all-hands meeting to address a critical issue on a project, would really love your input and advice before we all meet. Is it possible to talk tomorrow morning?"*

*On such short notice, it's rare to find me with an opening, but I knew it was a dire situation, so I gave her the only option I had. I told her we could meet at 8:00 a.m., but we generally met on FaceTime for our calls, so I told her that, in full disclosure, I would still be in "mommy-mode" taking care of my then-one-year-old, Dante, because the nanny wouldn't be arriving until later. As long as she was okay with this, we could take our chances and hopefully my son would be in his high chair eating breakfast at that time so he'd be quiet and occupied while she and I talked. If luck was not on our side and he was having a meltdown of some sort, we'd have to call it off.*

*"I'll take it," she replied.*

*At 8:00 the next morning the FaceTime application on my phone rang and I turned on the video. I was sitting in my kitchen, feeding the baby, wearing a tee-shirt, my hair pulled back in a pony tail. I told her that so far everything was under control, Dante was happily eating, and we could talk.*

*"Oh, is he there?" she asked with a smile. "Can I see him?"*

*"Sure," I said, and adjusted the camera angle. There she was, face to face with the big blue eyes of my son, with oatmeal on his*

*face, who greeted her with a squeal (he loves seeing people—and himself—on video) and a big, gummy grin showing all four teeth. She returned the gesture in the best way possible: by immediately launching into full-scale peek-a-boo mode, and was rewarded with more giggles and smiles.*

*After a moment or two, I turned the camera back towards myself so we could get down to business as planned. She sighed with a smile, and said, "This was the perfect start to my morning. It's the antidote to all the stress this project is causing. Thank you so much!" And with that, we got to work.*

Now, I want to reiterate, this is *not* how I typically run my coaching calls. But in the moment, we both understood the stakes, and I chose to take a calculated risk: letting her see a different, private side of me. It was a moment of vulnerability for me. Fortunately, the timing was good, my son cooperated, and in the end, the trust I extended to my client served to strengthen the bond between us that much more. We saw each other as people, two working mothers with shared personal and professional experiences.

As these tools become the norm in the workplace, it is crucial to be mindful of how you show up and how you communicate when using them. Your choices will determine what impact you have and either strengthen or weaken your ability to have the kind of influence you truly want, and it's important to be judicious. For example, I have had video conference meetings where I was interviewing prospective interns. Some were in sweatshirts, as if because they hadn't come to see me at my office and were just in their dorm rooms, their physical appearance didn't matter. In my opinion it certainly did, and it didn't help their case.

**Your choices will determine what impact you have and either strengthen or weaken your ability to have the kind of influence you truly want, so it's important to be judicious.**

Ultimately, the context in which you engage your target audience needs to be one of the primary filters through which you view your messaging. What appears to be in alignment in one context will not necessarily have a similar effect in another. Your ability to read each situation, the people, the purpose, and the goals and then to respond accordingly in the moment will be a critical factor in determining the quantity and quality of your influence on the outcome.

## VIII. POINTS OF IMPACT

1. These strategies and skills matter in all contexts, not just in formal speaking engagements. It's just a question of how to *apply* them in each.
2. Your reputation is what happens in the moments when you're not trying.
3. Public speaking is any time you're talking to someone other than yourself.
4. Introversion and extroversion are not predictors of comfort or skill in public speaking.
5. The "Sixty to Sixty" Rule: What you say and how you say it in the first sixty seconds will set people's expectations for what else you might provide in the next sixty minutes.
6. When preparing a slide deck, it is important to decide whether its purpose is to be used as a report to be read independently, or as part of a presentation, in which you (or someone else) will be the presenter. Just because something is in PowerPoint format doesn't mean it's an effective "presentation." When in doubt, have TWO versions, one for each setting.
7. Be the star of the show; let your slides be your "Backup." Keep your slides simple, then provide detail, story, and explanation. Remember: Don't be a Pip!
8. If you want to be heard and to create your own ideal leadership image at the same time, *diplomacy is critical.*
9. You need to apply all of these principles, bearing in mind your context: For example, will you be speaking to your audience in person or virtually? Will the conference call be by telephone only, or

will you also use video? Is it a two-minute networking conversation, or a two-hour meeting? Strategic framing and delivery will always get you closer to your goal.

# IX. BLIND SPOT CHALLENGE: CONSIDER YOUR CONTEXTS

Look at your calendar for the next week. Make a list of how many entries fall within each of the contexts identified in this chapter. For each item on your list, ask yourself and note:

- *What media will I use? (For example, will you have a slide deck, and is the goal to use the deck as a report, or as a visual aid during a presentation?)*
- *Are my slides presenter- and audience-friendly, based on my previous answer?*
- *In which conversations will I need to be particularly diplomatic? How should I plan to do that?*
- *What role should I take, and how can I maximize the value I bring and the value I take from that encounter?*
- *Considering my Prismatic Voice as discussed in Chapter 6, which of my "colors" should I let shine most brightly in each situation in order to make the right impact?*
- *Do I have any networking opportunities? If so, how can I get the most value from those experiences?*

Remember: The way you navigate every conversation, every day, matters. As Benjamin Franklin said, "Failing to plan is planning to fail." (He wasn't a character in Wonderland, but his point is still apropos nonetheless.)

# CHAPTER 8

## LISTENING TO INFLUENCE

*'I have answered three questions, and that is enough,'*
*Said his father; 'don't give yourself airs!*
*Do you think I can listen all day to such stuff?*
*Be off, or I'll kick you down stairs!'*
—Lewis Carroll. *Alice's Adventures in Wonderland.*

## I.  INTRODUCTION

When exploring issues such as leadership, communication, and influence, there's one factor that is easy to forget: communication is a two-way street. If you want people to truly hear you when you speak, more often than not, they first need to feel *heard* and *understood*. That means *you* have to listen to *them*.

## II.  WHEN TO STOP TALKING

Up until now, we've been focusing on identifying the best strategy, approach, or delivery to get your message through to your audience and get to "Yes." Now, however, I want to focus on the exact opposite skill set: knowing when and how to *stop* talking.

Self-awareness and emotional intelligence are critical here. You'll know when to stop talking when you see signs that indicate your audience is less than captivated, like when their eyes start to glaze over or more and more people are looking at their mobile phones. No matter how important *you* believe your message is, you have lost their attention. Once you realize that you have hit this point, you have two choices:

- ◾ Continue going down the "rabbit hole"—you prepared your presentation, and you need to finish it, regardless of whether or not anyone is listening, or
- ◾ Stop, acknowledge the situation, and *redirect your approach* and *efforts.* (Spoiler alert: The latter is more effective.)

---

*In the 1995 movie "Mr. Holland's Opus," Mr. Holland, a high school music teacher played by Richard Dreyfuss, is frustrated with his students. They are disengaged, slumped down in their chairs, yawning...a teacher's (and speaker's) worst nightmare. He opens class one day by asking a question from the homework, and doesn't even get eye contact from the students, much less an answer. He might have a command of the subject matter, but he is not commanding the room.*

*It finally dawns on him that the students aren't the problem, nor is the content. HE is the problem: he hasn't been listening. Because he has made them plod mechanically through the music theory textbook in class day in and day out, mentally, his students have all checked out. The deafening silence of the class is daily evidence that they aren't connecting with him or with what he is trying to teach. If he wants to get through to them, he has to change his approach.*

*Mr. Holland then sits down at the piano and starts playing popular rock and roll tunes that demonstrate examples of the musical structures described in the text book. The energy of the class shifts immediately. Students sit upright, smile, move in their seats to the music, and become absorbed in the discussion, fully engaged for the first time. He and the students get exactly what they want.*

---

By "redirecting your approach," I'm not suggesting you need to make every conversation fun. The point is that when you are trying to influence someone's thoughts, feelings, and behaviors, as I have mentioned previously in this book: *it's not about you.* The more you talk, the more you *make* it about you. But if you really want to connect with your audience and engage them fully and positively, you can't just be a good speaker. You have to be an excellent *listener.*

> **If you really want to connect with your audience**
> **and engage them fully and positively,**
> **you can't just be a good speaker.**
> **You have to be an excellent *listener*.**

## III.  FEAR OF SILENCE

Ironically, for many people, listening is the hardest part. If you're like me, when you're in a high-pressure situation, at some point or other you've had the "out-of-body experience," and as you catch yourself rambling on, your brain is screaming, "For heaven's sake, stop talking already!" But you've already gone tumbling down the rabbit hole and there is no end in sight.

Part of the reason this happens is because Americans in general (and American business culture in particular), are notoriously *uncomfortable* with silence in conversation. (Many other cultures share this discomfort as well.) Silence can quickly degrade to "awkward silence," which feeds the common compulsion to fill any silence at all costs.

In the vast majority of these occurrences, self-doubt is a huge factor. Even if you were confident up to that point, something triggers a sudden insecurity, consciously or subconsciously, which you telegraph through rambling.

With that in mind, let's look at a few contexts in which you are likely to slide into this "rambling mode," why, and how to get everything back under control, so you can navigate the conversation safely and successfully steer it wherever you want it to go, silences and all.

## A.  Non-Response

One of the most common kinds of uncomfortable silence is when you've asked a question or made a comment, and the other person doesn't respond right away. Your subconscious assumes they didn't understand what you said, or it panics—maybe they did understand, but didn't like it and don't want to reply. So, you rephrase ... or qualify ... or offer possible answers to your own question ... until they finally jump in and give a concrete response.

In reality, sometimes people just need a moment to digest what you've said. The more technical, important, complicated, or unknown a concept is to your audience, the more processing time they need. Be generous. Allow them time to think, uninterrupted, before they respond.

## B.   Thinking that More is Better

The second context in which you may slide into rambling mode is when you think you need to keep explaining something:

- ▩ Perhaps your topic is complicated. For example, if you are in the finance department and you are trying to make a point to your counterpart in marketing or IT who are not finance experts, you might think more details and examples will be helpful or even necessary for them to understand.
- ▩ You might be presenting an analysis to other experts such as your immediate supervisor (which can be intimidating), so you feel compelled to share every data point to demonstrate the extent of your knowledge and how hard you've worked on the project. Or...
- ▩ You might be pitching your idea to a high-stakes audience, such as a major client or potential investors, and interpret their silence as disapproval...at which point you keep talking in an attempt to qualify or justify your argument and persuade them to agree with you.

Ironically, however, in these situations, the more you talk, the more you will either overwhelm and confuse the non-expert, or dissuade your audience. Your rambling likely sounds nervous and uncertain rather than confident. In these cases, make your point, then hold your ground—and your tongue. This signals that you expect a response, and that it's *their* turn to break the silence. If necessary, calmly ask your audience if they are confused by something, or would like an example or further clarification. Knowing when to stop is a sign of confidence.

## C.   Thinking Aloud – Do's and Don'ts

Rambling also tends to occur when you need to answer a question or offer a response, and don't feel like you have time to think it through before you are expected to speak. The pressure is on. All eyes are on you. Each second of silence feels like an hour. But rather than taking your listeners on a stream-of-consciousness journey as you figure out what you want to say, try prefacing with something like, "That's a great question; let me think about the best way to answer it concisely." Then, jot down a few key ideas to help you organize your response. Who would deny that request, especially if the alternative is a rambling mess?

Here's a final tip: Write a note to remind yourself not to fall into these traps—even something as simple as a symbolic "X" on a Post-It note—and put it somewhere you will see it before you enter your next high stakes meeting. If you wait until you catch yourself mid-ramble, it's too late. You've gone down the rabbit hole, and there's no easy way back. Priming yourself with these reminders before you start is one of the best ways to project persuasive confidence and authority.

# IV.   LISTENING TO UNDERSTAND

Sometimes, however, you need to stop talking for another reason: so other people get the chance to speak and be heard. It's easy to forget that communication is a two-way street. As the saying goes, "That's why we have two ears and one mouth: so we can listen twice as much as we talk." Giving others time and space to share their thoughts, and truly *listening* to them with the right mindset and skill set is just as important—and often just as difficult—as learning to express your own thoughts effectively.

But effective listening goes beyond simply putting tape over your mouth. It begins with another critical mindset shift.

One of the biggest mistakes you can make in a conversation is making it your objective to "win." It's easy to fall into the habit of listening for the primary purpose of figuring out where you can interrupt, contradict, or reassert your own point. At the first opportunity, you might interject with "Yeah, but..." because your goal is simply to make the other person understand why you're right and they're wrong. This is what I call "listening to win."

## One of the biggest mistakes you can make is "listening to win."

When either or both people are listening to win, you can practically see the cartoon-like thought bubbles over their heads, all of which read, "You're not listening to me!" No matter how loudly you yell or how long you filibuster, it won't get you the big-picture results you want.

When your objective is *listening to win*, there are only two possible outcomes:

- both people in the interaction become frustrated and no solution or resolution is reached, or
- there is, in the moment, a "winner" and a "loser," where one person dominates the conversation and effectively forces the other person to concede or to accept their point of view.

In the end, though, everybody still loses, because there are repercussions. Morale, commitment, effort, loyalty, and relationships all suffer as a result.

Ask yourself: "Do I need to be right all the time? Do I need to prove everyone else wrong?" That means anytime you are in a disagreement with someone, the only way you will allow that person to walk away is to accept their status as *a loser*.

Think about it. Is that the kind of dynamic you want with your team, your family, or with other relationships? Will people feel they can have important and difficult conversations with you, knowing that if you disagree, their only choice is to tell you that you are right? Of course not.

How do you find the balance? What is the alternative? The alternative is *listening to understand*. Now this may sound simple at first glance, but simple things are not necessarily easy. Let's look at a few techniques to ensure you employ and promote active listening throughout your organization.

In listening to understand, first you need to put aside all of your assumptions. It's so easy to walk into conversations thinking, "I know what he is going to say. He says it all the time. I just need to tell him why he's wrong." This is counterproductive.

Instead, accept the fact that if the other party is still fighting you on something, *you probably are missing something important*. Ask yourself:

- What is it about their priorities, values, or concerns that is creating the road block?
- Is there a competing priority?
- Is there pressure coming from somewhere else that's forcing them to dig their heels in?
- What is the nature of their resistance?

Shift your focus. Accept that there is information you do not have, so it is your job in this conversation to figure out what that is, through listening to understand. Then and only then can you make progress.

## A. Establishing Safety

Part of the challenge of achieving this goal of filling in the missing piece and listening to understand is that other people might be unwilling to tell you the truth, for many possible reasons. Ultimately, any hesitation on their part to truly engage in discussion with you, fully and freely, is based on the feeling of a *lack of safety*.

Let's say you need to have a conversation with Ralph, your direct report. Ralph has a track record of missing deadlines. You have told him in the past that if he realizes he might miss another, he needs to alert you immediately so you and the team can adjust expectations or shift your own efforts accordingly. He always agrees to do so in the future, but inevitably does not follow through.

For Ralph to be willing to open up and share potentially sensitive information, he needs to know it is safe to tell you the truth. Particularly since there is a power differential, he needs to be reassured unambiguously that he has full permission to share his thoughts (respectfully) without fear of repercussion.

How can you do this? State outright that you will not shoot the messenger...and then *follow through on that promise*. Whether it's because Ralph disagrees with your plan of action, has so much on his plate that it's literally impossible for him to meet the deadlines imposed on him, or needs to talk with you about one of *your* habits that is having a negative impact on his ability to perform optimally, consider the options. Which is worse:

- Should he tell you only what he thinks you want to hear, letting reality fester behind the scenes until the problem is so big that it can no longer be ignored?
- Or should he tell you something you won't like now, but which will allow you to take appropriate measures to prevent irreparable damage in the future?

Ralph has an important decision to make, and it shouldn't be the choice between what is in the company's best interest and his own job security, despite the fact that his job may be at stake anyway if his track record doesn't improve.

This is Ralph's opportunity to demonstrate leadership by "managing up" with you, speaking his truth to your power, and being willing to be—even momentarily—unpopular because he sees the need and takes responsibility for revealing unpopular facts. But to be able to do this, Ralph needs you to encourage and demonstrate these behaviors.

This is also an opportunity for you to model what kind of culture you want to establish within your team and organization—and that culture is established in great part by how you handle conflict. Of course, regardless of your claims of openness, speaking through barred teeth and with clenched fists wouldn't exactly project the alignment necessary to take your invitation for a free, truthful, and *safe* exchange of information as sincere and credible. Modeling the delivery of such invitations will be just as critical as extending them in the first place.

> **Model what kind of culture you want to establish within your team and organization by how you handle conflict.**

## B.  Note-Taking and Active Listening

Once you have established that Ralph can safely engage in conversation with you, without fear of consequences, one of the simplest and most powerful ways to establish trust is to *invite him to talk first*. Showing that you are willing to listen first can be disarming—because most people aren't! The security in knowing that he will get a chance to share his thoughts, combined with proof that you actually hear and understand them when he does, will help Ralph to be open to whatever *you* may say later.

What kind of evidence serves as valid proof? First, as you're listening, try taking notes. Have a pen and paper ready to jot down key ideas as necessary. Don't take notes on your phone...it is too tempting to "multitask," checking messages and the like, which only proves that you are *not* listening. For that matter, even if you truly are just taking notes on your phone, it *looks* like you might be multitasking, which casts doubt on your sincerity, and sabotages your purpose for starting the conversation.

"Why take notes at all," you ask? For a number of reasons:

- It helps you remember what Ralph said so you can refer back to your list later in the conversation with greater accuracy. I'm not suggesting you take dictation or formal meeting minutes, but when something sticks out to you, make a brief note.
- Make a note to yourself if there is something you want to add or questions you want to ask. As Ralph keeps talking, you're probably going to hear a variety of points that you want to address, such as misperceptions you want to correct, or additional information you want to give him. Jot down your ideas and questions so you don't lose your thought when it's your turn to talk later.
- Not only does note-taking allow you to remember what you wanted to say, it keeps you from interrupting—again, a courtesy most people are *not* used to receiving! Occasional interruptions to ask Ralph to repeat something you couldn't hear, clarify something you didn't understand, or perhaps missed because you were writing something else are acceptable, of course. Otherwise, hold your feedback and additional questions until he is done.

Patience pays off. As Ralph has the opportunity to share more, there is a high probability he will answer some of the questions that had come into your mind before you even had a chance to ask them. You can cross those items off your notes list and not waste time: problem solved. It also allows you time to digest his message, both the big-picture and small details, organizing and prioritizing your own thoughts before you speak. All of these steps contribute to establishing trust and credibility, and keeping the conversation focused and effective.

## 1. Listen Patiently

Part of the challenge in listening to understand is that when people talk—especially under emotionally-charged circumstances—they are not always logical and organized. It's sort of stream-of-conscious venting. Everything that has been bottled up is coming to the surface as it occurs to them, which can make it difficult to figure out where they are going with their comments. Nevertheless, unless you're really confused by something (in which case do interrupt to ask for clarification), try not to ask questions seeking much more detail at this stage because there is a good chance Ralph will get around to providing the information on his own.

## 2. Avoid Premature Judgment

Additionally, remember that even though you are not communicating verbally (i.e., through words), you *are* communicating vocally and visually, so be careful! You may be taking notes and letting Ralph talk, but if you sigh repeatedly, groan, roll your eyes, or shake your head, that's not *active* listening. Instead of taking in the information and analyzing it objectively, your body and voice are telegraphing exactly how you feel, and indicating that you've already cast judgment. (Nobody wants to present a case to the Queen in Wonderland, whose order of operation is: "Sentence first—verdict afterwards.")

**Nobody wants to present a case to the Queen in Wonderland, whose order of operation is: "Sentence first—verdict afterwards."**

## 3. Resist Point-Counterpoint

There is one important pitfall to avoid when note-taking, even if you *can* do it with a poker face. Your notes are *not* to be used for arguing point-counterpoint against every detail the person mentioned.

> *I had to correct this mistake with my client, Marissa, who was notoriously detail-oriented. She took my original suggestion and tried note-taking during a meeting with Karl, an under-performing employee. But instead of using her notes to SEEK clarification, she used them to shoot holes in his argument, pointing out every inaccurate or missing detail in what Karl had said. As a result, what should have been a twenty- to thirty-minute conversation lasted two and a half hours! By the end, both were frustrated and exhausted, and I'm sure Karl was demoralized as well.*
>
> *Needless to say, this sabotaged Marissa's goal of learning to listen to understand. She listened for the sake of destroying Karl's argument, as proof of all the ways that he was wrong and she was right. That does not establish an environment of safety or collaboration, and, if anything, would condition him to decline any future invitation to speak for fear of a repeat experience.*

Ultimately, you have to make a choice: To address everything on your list superficially, or pick the most important issues and focus on arriving at a mutually agreeable resolution. The goal is to clarify the big picture, identifying and prioritizing the most important points the two of you need to discuss if you want to make any real progress. Done right, you may find that if you can resolve the top priority issues, the little ones won't matter anymore, or will be much easier to handle afterwards.

## C.  Mirroring

Once you've taken those notes, as difficult as it may be to hold most of your comments until Ralph is done speaking, you can segue: *Thank* him for sharing. Remember, it is important that he feels *safe*, which includes feeling acknowledged, appreciated, and validated. Explain that now that you've listened to his ideas or concerns, you'd like to check and make sure you understood them correctly.

Try something along the lines of, "I'd like to confirm what I think I heard you say. Please tell me if I have misunderstood anything and correct it as necessary, okay?" This disrupts Ralph's defenses because it is not how he had anticipated the conversation going, since few people ever take the time to do it. Most prefer to launch into, "Now it's my turn to talk, so here's why you're wrong...." By rhetorically asking for permission to check your understanding, it gets him to say "Yes." It also makes him curious, and open to this part of the discussion. After all, who would say "No" to a request like that?

This is when you will begin *mirroring*. In mirroring, you merely summarize and paraphrase what you understood to be Ralph's key points. Just as a mirror shows you exactly what you look like, without interpretation or judgment, you will reflect back to Ralph objectively what you heard him say.

In mirroring, you want to use reporting language, including phrases like, "You said that you want more feedback, positive and negative, on your work. Is that correct?" Keep your statements objective, reporting no more and no less than what his main points were, whether or not you like or agree with any of them. You need to be able to say, objectively and calmly, "Your complaint is X, your concern is Y, your request is Z. Did I get that right?" Remember, your goal is for Ralph to feel he has been heard and understood. So, although you are talking now, it is still a part of actively listening.

When you are mirroring, do not try to interpret or read meaning into anything Ralph said. For example, do *not* say things like, "So it sounds like you don't think I pay enough attention to you." In mirroring, you're only feeding back to him what *you think* he said, even if you think it's the dumbest thing you've heard all day. If he insists that the moon is made of cheese, confirm that you heard him accurately: "You said the moon is made of cheese. Did I hear that correctly?"

One crucial caveat here is that it's not just your words that have to be neutral and objective. If you confirm Ralph's belief about the moon being made of cheese but with a smirk on your face, with one incredulous eyebrow cocked, or using a snide or mocking tone, he'll pick up on it. It will sabotage the rest of your efforts for one core reason: it implies an inherent lack of respect for both the speaker and the idea. The entire point of these protocols is to establish a foundation of mutual respect, through listening, to allow people to open up and engage in productive dialogue and problem-solving. Once that respect is gone, the rest of the framework crumbles.

**It's not just your words that have to be neutral and objective.
Your voice and body language do too.**

Assuming you have reflected Ralph's words and meaning back to him with the right delivery, mirroring his key points gives him a chance to adjust and clarify his story as well. At this point, there may be some back-and-forth... perhaps he needs to clarify something, either because you misheard (maybe because you had temporarily zoned out at that moment!) or because he misspoke. If he says something like, "No, what I said was that it was made of *blue* cheese," or "Well, yes, I guess that's what I said but what I meant was that it just *looks* like the moon is made of cheese," *good!* This gives him a chance to realize where *he* wasn't clear, perhaps because he was speaking emotionally but not carefully or accurately when he blurted something out. The result of this step is that you don't end up wasting time debating a point he either didn't make or didn't mean to make in the first place.

However, if he corrects himself, you need to accept the change, and you can't hold the original misstatement against him later. To keep the discussion focused and productive, stick with what he has clarified as his intended meaning and forget the rest.

## D. Building Understanding Together

Once you and Ralph are in agreement that you have understood his perspective, switch roles. As you shift from objectively reporting what he said to making your own contributions, an important tool to include at the transition (as well as later where possible) is to explicitly *acknowledge and validate* something he said before launching into your side of the story. You don't have to pretend to agree with everything he said, but it is important as a "social lubricant" to let him know that you do appreciate and recognize the validity and value of (at least some of) his contributions.

Comments such as, "I can see where it would be very frustrating for you when..." or "I agree with your concern about..." *establish common ground.* They let Ralph hear the most disarming message ever: "You're right."

In the theater world, there's a popular improvisation game called "Yes, and," in which participants have to accept and build on whatever their partner says. "No, but" is not allowed, no matter how ridiculous or poorly thought-out a comment might be. The idea is that "yes, and" keeps momentum in a conversation whereas "no" and/or "but" immediately shuts it down. Of course, in real life, the ultimate answer is often "no," but when it starts with a "yes, and" kind of approach, it lands quite differently.

I'm not saying you have to be a "yes-man" or hold back from correcting any misconceptions the other person may have shared. The idea is to start with the mindset of openness and promote two-way openness by helping the other person feel not only heard but understood. For example, the statement "No, you can't have the salary increase you're asking for" will be received differently if it starts from, "Yes, I know you have worked hard and made great progress; I don't want you to think it has gone unnoticed. I want to be able to give you the raise. There are a few challenges that get in the way of my ability to do that at this moment...." If you go with the former, the discussion will likely come to a screeching halt and grudge-related repercussions may become a new "normal" in your relationship. Opting for the latter (yes, and) allows the flow to continue without negative effect on the conversation or relationship.

Now, as you prepare to share your side of the story, it's your turn to help Ralph listen to understand. As you move into this phase, you can segue with something simple like, "Alright, I'm glad you feel heard and understood; that's important to me. From there, I'd like to share some additional information that might shed some light on the situation."

## 1.   *Staying Neutral*

When you are giving your information, it is imperative to use—and encourage Ralph to use—neutral and objective language. Saying, "Now that I understand what your major concerns are, I think it will help if I share some information your team may not be aware of yet," sounds *very* different from, "You clearly don't know what you're talking about! Here's where you're wrong...."

The first version is neutral in tone; you are simply identifying an information gap and offering to fill it. The second might more accurately reflect what you are actually *thinking* and *want* to say, especially if you've heard some emotionally-charged complaints or accusations coming at you. Of course, it's also antagonistic, and unlikely to help promote productive discussion.

Occasionally, using grammatical *passive voice* can be more diplomatic and easier to hear. For example, you could say, "There's some additional information *you may not have been made aware of*," which removes any implication of blame. In contrast, "You don't know anything about X" is practically guaranteed to make someone's defenses go up—instead of attacking the argument itself, it is a direct attack on the person.

## 2.  *Promoting a Culture of Listening to Understand*

Before you start to share your side of the story, you may also need to teach Ralph the active listening steps by pointing out to him the steps you took when he was speaking. For example, you might say, "You may have noticed I held my main questions and comments until the end. I would appreciate it if you could do the same for me. Then I'm happy to answer any questions you have, and listen to your additional thoughts. Here's some paper and a pen for you to jot down anything you like so you don't forget what you want to say." That way there is a clearly specified and shared expectation for behavioral protocols that is reciprocal and respectful.

Be prepared for some resistance. For example:

- Even if Ralph declines the paper and dismisses your suggestion, saying, "I don't need to take notes," leave the paper and pen at arm's length so he can grab it easily if he changes his mind (which is likely to happen—as you're talking, something will pop into his mind that he won't want to forget).
- As you are talking, if he starts to interject with a "Yeah, but…," you can stop, smile gently, and say, "I do want to hear what you have to say, and if there's an issue, great, let's talk about it, but again, please let me finish first." Of course, if he interrupts to ask you to repeat or clarify something, be sure to oblige patiently and kindly.

Keep your instructions and information neutral and unemotional, not robotic or annoyed. If you feel his emotions rising, keep yours even. Don't take the bait. Don't follow suit. Letting emotions take over is the equivalent of throwing a grenade into your conversation.

Once you have shared your side, filling in gaps and offering corrections or an alternative viewpoint where necessary, ask Ralph to *mirror* what he heard back to you using neutral, reporting language. To allay any concerns of skepticism, try something like:

- ◾ "That's all I wanted to share with you. Can you tell me what you understood my main points to be? I want to make sure I'm communicating effectively." This is your chance to help him build more active listening skills as well.
- ◾ Reassure him that this is *not a quiz*. You don't expect him to remember every sentence. Remind him that he doesn't have to agree with or even like everything (or anything) you said; you just need to confirm that he understood your main points, as you did for him. Then he'll have a chance to respond with his own information once again.

Repeat the cycle of listening to understand, taking notes as needed, mirroring and clarifying until all the necessary information is on the table. If you run out of time, schedule a time to resume the conversation, but don't shortcut the process if you want the best possible outcome of a clear and mutually-accepted resolution and a strong, healthy relationship.

## E.  Mutual Understanding and Acceptance

Once you've had a chance to get all the facts out in the open, you can start working towards collaboration. At this point, the answer could be "yes" due to the new, shared perspective, or you may even be able to identify new possibilities and options through a mutually-understood and complete set of facts.

However, even after the best dialogue and perspective exchange, sometimes the answer still has to be *no*. "No, I can't extend the deadline," or, "No, we don't have the budget to hire more people for this project." But when you are explaining it, you want to balance it with both objective and subjective language, in order to be as diplomatic as possible. Even more importantly, be ready to accept responsibility when necessary. For example:

- ◾ Start by subjectively empathizing with Ralph's situation: "I realize that it's frustrating when you have voiced concern about accepting certain projects and the department has gone ahead with them anyway. I can see how it would feel like adding insult to injury if your prediction comes true but you are still expected to handle it."

- Then objectively acknowledge the facts, such as, "There are really two issues here. First, I *do* understand that this situation of overcommitting has happened more than once, and that is one issue I will watch more carefully in the future. I can't promise the department will always follow your recommendation, but you and I will set more careful plans moving forward. That one is on me. The second pertains to how to deal with problem deadlines, whether or not you predicted them. Passive-aggressive choices like withholding communication about deadlines because you are angry about them are not acceptable because they punish everyone individually and the company as a whole. I realize and understand that you feel like your efforts at communication fell on deaf ears in the beginning, so let's figure out what kind of system to put in place so that you feel heard, along with accountability measures, to ensure communication stays open no matter what."

- Finally, bookend it with more subjective, personal statements of support and context, such as, "I realize we've been understaffed for a while, which has been particularly hard on you, and I wish I could tell you we're going to hire two more people, but right now I can't. But I also want to make sure you understand why, and get your commitment to communicating with me as promised. It's important to me that you feel like I understand where you're coming from; that you feel like you've been heard, understood, and respected, and that you understand where my hands are tied as well. Have we accomplished that today?"

This is critical because if you have gone through the process effectively, at the very least Ralph will feel heard and respected. He may not like the final answer he gets, but he will understand that it's not just because you're a callous jerk who doesn't care. It will allow both of you to maintain the balance between clarity of message and a healthy, mutually respectful relationship.

If this process is repeated regularly and intentionally, such productive exchanges will get easier and more efficient. More importantly, ultimately they will become part of the organizational culture in which everyone feels safe. They know that their message will be heard, and that others will make a sincere effort to hear what they have to say, which will positively influence every other aspect of your business.

> *These active-listening steps can be used within any relationship, personal or professional, whether on the phone, in person, or communicating via Skype or other video application. For example, when I was first married, my husband and I followed this routine regularly when we had a potentially sensitive issue to discuss, and it really helped us to establish the right dynamic in our family, which we also have used from time to time with our teenage son. Now, when one of us tries to engage the other in a conversation about a topic that could get heated, the other person's response is still occasionally, "Should we get some paper?"*

## F.   The Learning Curve

If your initial concern upon reading this chapter is that the process seems time-consuming, you're right: it *can* be, especially in the beginning as you are learning the skills and steps. The good news is that you get more efficient with practice, and it's worth its weight in gold when done right. The benefits it yields are measured in reduced stress, coming to mutually acceptable and accepted outcomes, and maintaining strong relationships, among other things. Plus, if the issue is not resolved to satisfaction the first time, how much *more* time will be wasted when you have to revisit the topic over and over again?

Listening to understand through active listening skills such as paraphrasing, using reporting language, and mirroring information objectively, without interpretation, judgment, or correction, is not something that can be mastered overnight. It takes practice and patience, so if you try it once and don't have a transformational experience, that doesn't mean it doesn't work. Think of it like learning to swim: You can't just read a book and expect to become a lifeguard—you have to practice. Similarly, I promise you, practicing listening to understand until you master it is worth it. For an easy reminder of the steps in listening to understand, see the "Listening to Influence" checklist in the Appendix and on the Supplemental Materials page on https://SpeakingToInfluence.com.

If you ignore the lessons laid out in this chapter you will, in many ways, sabotage the effectiveness of what you learn from the rest of the book. You can have a perfectly-crafted and expertly delivered message, but it's useless if nobody is listening to you. When people don't listen, often it is because they're used to feeling like other people don't listen to them...so the cycle continues. If you truly want to stop this cycle of futility, get others to listen by modeling for them how to do it first. Leading by example is the first step in converting minds and hearts.

**Get others to listen by modeling for them how to do it first.**

## V. POINTS OF IMPACT

1. Effective listening is as important in leadership and influence as effective speaking.
2. When someone isn't listening to you, there is a good chance it is because they don't feel like you are listening to them.
3. Don't be afraid of silence. Being comfortable with silence projects confidence and control.
4. Listen genuinely to understand the other party's perspective, not just to find a place to jump in and talk more.
5. For people to be willing to tell you the truth, they have to feel safe from repercussions if you don't like what they share.
6. When listening, take notes to remember key points and organize your thoughts, and to keep from interrupting.
7. Objectively reflect back what you hear the other person say, to confirm your understanding. Do *not* evaluate, judge, critique, or otherwise *comment* on it.

8. When adding new information, start by acknowledging their perspective first, then stay neutral and objective when sharing your own.
9. Check their understanding. Guide them to take notes, mirror, and confirm understanding, then clarify as needed.
10. If the final answer isn't a version of "yes," be diplomatic. Ensure that the other person understands your reasons, even if they don't like them. This helps you gain mutual perspective and maintain or strengthen relationships—no matter what the final outcome might be.

## VI. BLIND SPOT CHALLENGE

- Think about a time you found yourself rambling.
  - What do you think caused it?
  - At what point should you have stopped talking?
  - What could you have done instead?
- Think about a conversation you're going to have (or should have) with someone, where things might get uncomfortable because of a difference of perspective, or for other reasons. Set up the time to talk, and bring paper and a pen for both of you.
  - Review the steps outlined in this chapter for Listening to Understand and having difficult conversations.
  - Plan whatever key points you think you will want to address, to organize your thoughts. Remember that these may change once you hear the other person's side first.
  - Use these steps to establish safety, collect the facts, clarify, and reinforce the relationship while coming to a mutually accepted resolution.
  - Afterwards, reflect on the conversation:
    - What went according to plan? What surprised you? What was easier or more difficult than expected?
    - What lessons did you learn from this experience? About yourself? About the other person? About how to adopt and adapt this process with more people?
- Set new leadership listening goals for yourself.

# CHAPTER 9

## YOUR VOICE OF INFLUENCE - PUTTING IT ALL TOGETHER

*'I quite agree with you,' said the Duchess; 'and the moral of that is—'Be what you would seem to be....''*
—Lewis Carroll. *Alice's Adventures in Wonderland.*

## I.  LOVE WHAT YOU DO

I love my job.

I love the feeling of anticipation when I'm getting ready to speak to an audience. The little butterflies that start to flutter in my stomach as I hear the host giving my introduction are a happy reminder that I am excited to be there. I truly care about the attendees and I want them to leave smiling, feeling like they got more value out of our time together than they could have imagined and are glad they were there.

I'm confident in my content and excited at the opportunity to open more people's eyes, to help them suddenly see how they are holding themselves back, and how everything they need to be more influential and successful is right at their fingertips—or on the tip of their tongue, as the case may be.

When I look around the room, all eyes are looking back at me. Nobody is "multitasking," checking text messages or email on their phone. No one is being held captive; they're simply *captivated*. I have their full attention, and they're subconsciously committed to maximizing the value of our time together.

As the program goes on, I watch their heads nod as they process what I'm saying. The crowd laughs on cue, sometimes with a chuckle of appreciation, sometimes a full-scale belly laugh: a not-so-subtle confession that they relate 100 percent to the story I've just told. We're having fun—but I know it's hitting home.

Ideally, the activities—whether individual, pair work, or whole-group Q&A—hum with participation. Questions are sincere, curious, and sometimes challenging, which I love because it lets me know what matters most to the audience, and gives me a chance to go into greater depth on something they actively want to know more about. People are fully engaged, trusting that whatever time and effort they invest will yield a far greater return.

As we wrap up, I show a slide with my contact information and invite people to follow up with me and get a private breakthrough session. That's when the phones start to come out. Not because they've lost interest, but because they want to take a photo of the screen to ensure they capture the information correctly. If they've gotten that much out of a group program, they can imagine what's possible if we were to work together one-on-one.

In the end, everyone gets up...but few leave. They may have come at first because they were supposed to, but now they stay because they *want* to. There is an energetic buzz in the room as people continue to discuss their take-aways and observations with colleagues. A growing group of people joins me at the front of the room, wanting to ask more questions, share feedback, and inquire about follow-up opportunities to work together, whether through individual coaching, group training, or future speaking engagements.

As I pack up to go home, I'm tired, but energized, satisfied, and happy. Over the next few days, my email and then my calendar start to fill up with enthusiastic next steps.

And do you know what the best part of it all is?

*This could be YOU.*

As a matter of fact, it not only *could* be you, it *should* be you, it *can* be you, and it *will* be you, if you take to heart and practice what we've discussed in this book. And you and I both know that if you've stuck with me this far, it's because deep down you *want* it to be you, and you're committed to making it happen.

**It not only *could* be you, it *should* be you,**
**it *can* be you, and it *will* be you,**
**if you take to heart and practice what**
**we've discussed in this book.**

How, you ask? Let's start with a quick recap of our journey so far, where we started, and where we are now. Then we can determine the next steps for you to take so that, sooner rather than later, you can re-read that last scenario and envision a giant flashing yellow arrow pointing at it, which reads, "YOU ARE HERE."

## II.  LOOKING BACK

You started out with a problem: You're not getting the results you want. You can't get or keep key people's attention. Maybe they interrupt you or shoot down your ideas. If they listen, they still don't get it, or they understand generally what you're saying but they don't get *you*. There's a disconnect that's preventing you from having critical influence and being successful. You wanted to figure out what the cause was, and what you could do about it.

That's why in Chapter 1, we began by exploring the broad nature of leadership, not so much as a role or position, but as an image or perception that is irrespective of your official title. A true leader has an inherent, positive ability to influence and motivate others. Chapter 2 then provided an outline for understanding what creates a positive leadership image. This includes having a clear vision and being able to articulate it while demonstrating the Three Cs of vocal executive presence: *Command* the room, *Connect* with the audience, and *Close* the deal. It closed by laying out a framework for being in alignment when communicating with others in order to establish credibility, a cornerstone of leadership.

From there, Chapters 3, 4, and 5 each took one component from the alignment framework—verbal, vocal, and visual communication (i.e., your words, voice, and body language, respectively). They illustrated core factors that will either create or destroy your credibility through your speech.

Then in Chapter 6, we took a good, hard look at the identity mindset necessary to have maximum persuasion and influence. We explored the importance of balancing authenticity with the ability and willingness to expand your sense of identity, and flex your speaking style in order to meet the needs and expectations of different audiences. This is key to achieving your desired outcomes from those engagements.

Next, Chapter 7 put everything we had discussed into context. Whether giving a formal speech, talking on the telephone, participating in a weekly departmental meeting or having an informal networking conversation with someone over coffee, your communication approach makes a difference. Your mindset, words, voice, and body language need to work together to project the right image and leave the desired, lasting impact. If you don't take the context into consideration, you'll miss the mark.

Finally, in Chapter 8, we looked at the other side of the leadership communication coin: leadership through *listening*, rather than talking. For others to listen to you openly, it is of critical importance to lead by example and demonstrate how openly and sincerely *you* can listen to *them*. Through establishing that mutual respect for each other's perspective, you create a safe space where productive, constructive, and collaborative discussion can take place around any issue. Not only can you achieve mutually desirable results, but you can do it while maintaining and even *strengthening* the integrity of your relationship.

Now it's time to put it all into application and experience how these principles serve as tools for you to use in honing your own voice of influence. Just as every car has a blind spot when you drive it, every person has his or her own blind spot when talking. As I have said from the start, my job is to help you identify and close that very important gap: The gap between how you *want* to come across, how you *think* you come across, and how you *actually* come across to others when you speak. That's the blind spot. Until the ego gets out of the way and you have both the tools and the willingness to look for it, this gap will continue to undermine your goals, influence, and impact.

The good news is that if you've gotten this far, you clearly have the willingness, and now you have the tools. Now it's time to put those tools to work and close that gap.

## III. THE THREE CS IN PRACTICE

Command the room. Connect with the audience. Close the deal. Sounds simple enough, doesn't it? Actually, *it is*. Once again, just because something is *simple* doesn't mean it's easy, of course. At the same time, however, it's not as difficult as you might think. With each little principle you apply, you turn the dial another notch in your favor and tap further into the source of your true leadership image and powers of influence.

What's critical to remember is that the Three Cs don't just matter when you're running the show, on stage, or on camera. They matter every bit as much when you're one of the group, and even if you're "low man on the totem pole." They merely require a little forethought and planning, as we discussed in Chapter 2.

> **The Three Cs don't just matter when you're running the show... They even matter if you're "low man on the totem pole."**

For example, one afternoon I was in a department meeting over at the University of Pennsylvania, where I was teaching a few graduate classes. At the meeting, there were about twenty people around the table, all in different roles. Some of them I was meeting for the first time, some I'd known for years. I was supposed to lead one part of the meeting, sharing the progress that had been made that semester in a small program I was building, with the goal of getting approval for additional support and funding for the following year.

Now, this was a challenge for several reasons. I was a non-tenured, part-time faculty member. As such, I did not rank highly on the academic totem pole...as a matter of fact, I would probably have ranked *under* the totem pole, if that were possible. I was neither invited to nor permitted to attend regular department meetings, and I was only at this one because of the update I was to provide. As far as most people there were concerned, they knew I came in to teach a class or two each week, then left. They had no idea (or inherent interest) regarding what I did with the rest of my life. As a result, most did not know that I have a consulting business, or more specifically that I do training and coaching related to leadership communication and the like. They just knew which classes I taught, and were only peripherally aware of or interested in the related program I was trying to build.

That's why, when I was preparing to share the updates, I knew that I didn't want the department to gloss over it with a generic "good job." I needed them to understand the current and intended reach of the program. I wanted them to recognize my passion for the program, the magnitude of its potential impact, and my ability to take it to the next level if given the necessary resources. I needed them to take it seriously...which means I needed them to take *me* seriously.

While I wasn't melodramatic, I made sure that no matter who they were or where anyone was sitting, they heard what I was saying, and felt like I was talking directly to them. I chose my words carefully, articulated them deliberately, and allowed my body language to reinforce their meaning purposefully.

At the meeting, there was one new senior faculty member whose work I had admired for a long time. When the meeting ended, I went over to introduce myself to her. After exchanging initial greetings, the first thing she said to me was, "You know, you're a very good speaker."

Since she knew nothing about me other than what was shared in the meeting, I found it particularly interesting that her first comment to me pertained to my speaking style. It stuck with me, so the next day I sent her a brief email to follow up. In it, I thanked her for her generous comment and asked if she would mind describing what had prompted her to say it.

In her reply, she wrote, "Here are my two cents'/four sentences' worth: You spoke with confidence and authority. You made your point—sometimes humorously—in a succinct manner. You swept the room with your gaze. You have a mellifluous speaking voice."

Notice that she didn't talk about how powerful or dynamic I sounded. There was no drama involved. However, she did explicitly address exactly one verbal, one vocal, and one visual factor, along with one overall presence factor. I wasn't "presenting," per se, or showing off. If it had seemed like I was, she probably wouldn't have offered the compliment in the first place. Without intending to do so, she confirmed that I was in complete alignment when I spoke, and she found it clear, authoritative, and compelling.

And for the record, in spite of wider budgetary challenges, I got the funding and support I needed to expand the program the following year. Despite my lack of official leadership status based on the hierarchy of those present, I had commanded the room, connected with the audience, and closed the deal.

It's that simple. Now, I'm not saying you'll get everything you want all the time just because you make these changes, but you *will* make that strong and positive of an impression. People *will* pay attention when you speak, and they *will* hear not only what you say, but what you mean, and understand why it should matter to them. One way or another, this *will* positively influence the short- and long-term outcome.

Plus, once you get used to putting the Three Cs into practice in smaller, less formal contexts, it will start to become second nature, your "new normal." Then it's much easier to implement in higher stakes situations when the pressure is really on.

So, where should you start?

## IV. FEEDBACK AND FEED FORWARD

I've had the honor and the pleasure of working with thousands of people through coaching, training, and speaking engagements, and millions of viewers have seen my TEDx talk. As part of my own ongoing efforts at self-improvement and program development, I regularly solicit feedback at the end of an engagement. I also get lots of unsolicited feedback, whether via email or because people stick around to speak with me after an event. There are a few key themes that pop up in the majority of comments I receive, which I will share with you here ("feed forward"), as I believe they will help you to make important choices in creating your leadership image.

### A. Small Details Make a Big Difference

It could be the way you say your own name when you introduce yourself, the eye contact you make with your audience, or your ability to illustrate your point with a little story. But whether you do these things consciously or subconsciously, people will notice the difference and it will influence the way they respond to you.

I've had countless people tell me that they changed the outbound message on their voicemail system after hearing me speak. One person, Dean, recently shared that by changing the way he pronounced his full name when introducing himself, people no longer asked him to repeat it when he introduces himself on the phone. Another, Martin, said he was suddenly clear on what was causing the tension between his wife and teenage son, and it was all about how conversations *sounded* when they started, regardless of their topic.

Regardless of what kind of influence you need to gain or with whom, personally or professionally, the principles outlined in this book work. Don't worry about mastering all the skills right away. Take it one step at a time, and trust that each step makes its own impact.

## B.  It's Not Just About Communication—*It's About Strategy*

Going back to the Cheshire Cat's advice (or lack thereof) at the start of this book, in order to influence a situation and get the results you want, you need a plan. It needs to start with choosing your desired reputation and outcome, followed by an intentional approach for how to get there, verbally, vocally, and visually. As one CFO with whom I worked said, "It's more than language. I learned to think and speak more strategically. That was the key."

## C.  Be Willing *to Step Out of Your Comfort Zone*

One of my favorite evaluation forms came from Ben, a participant in a multi-day, intensive training program I ran for a large non-profit organization. Over the course of several days, attendees did a *lot* of video recording of themselves speaking on different topics, and even more analysis of the videos. Ben was a self-proclaimed, painfully shy introvert who hated speaking in public, much less on camera, but made huge strides in his overall leadership presence in those few days. To his credit, his semi-facetious comment at the bottom of the evaluation form on the last day was, "I hated every minute of this. Thank you for making me do it. Need more."

## D.   Practice Makes Perfect, and *Recording Yourself During Practice Is Essential*

Piggy-backing on the previous point, I will almost never give a client feedback on their speech unless we've recorded an excerpt that we can go back and review together. This is for one crucial reason: The recording—whether video or just audio, depending on the context—eliminates your blind spot.

### Recording yourself—whether video or just audio— eliminates your blind spot.

Remember that the blind spot is the gap between how you *want* to come across, how you *think* you come across, and how you *actually* come across when you speak. When you talk, you have certain assumptions about the quality of your performance, for better or for worse. If I try to give you constructive feedback, your brain goes into what I call "deny-and-defend mode." That's where your reflex is often to dismiss or downplay my comments, rationalizing that I must have missed what you were trying to say, or that something wasn't as serious as I claimed.

When you watch the video, however, you see *exactly* what I saw, and hear *exactly* what I heard. One recent workshop participant, Sara, watched her own video and exclaimed, "I can't believe my left arm never moved the entire time! My right arm was waving all over the place, but the left one just sat there as if it was taped to my body—and I'm a professional speaker! I had no idea!"

Another participant, Sheila, realized that her outbound voicemail message was peppered with up-speak, sounding like a litany of questions from start to finish. ("Hi, this is Sheila? I'm sorry I missed your call? But if you leave your name and number?...") She re-recorded it, listened again, and blurted out, "Oh my gosh, I specifically re-recorded it so that it *wouldn't* be full of up-speak, and I *still* did it!"

On the other hand, sometimes your blind spot is in the opposite direction: You think you come across much *worse* than you actually do. (After all, we can all be our own worst critic.) At those times, the recording shows that the depth of your fears was unwarranted.

Barbara, another workshop participant, said, "I absolutely dreaded making the video, but after I watched it I was relieved. It actually was pretty good, and I realized I'm not so bad at this after all. It gave me confidence." Although there is always room for improvement, the video can enable you to relax a bit, speak with more confidence, and stop beating yourself up for no reason.

One way or another, the recording provides the objectivity and perspective to recognize the gap between your intention and your execution (the blind spot), the impression that you made, and the likely effect you would have. If you record yourself, there's a good chance you won't even need me to give you certain kinds of feedback, because you'll be crystal-clear on what worked in your favor, what didn't, and why. You might just want some guidance on how to improve.

## V. FINAL THOUGHTS

Although it's not often seen on feedback forms, there is one final piece of advice I'd like to share. As you go through the learning curve of trying to make some of these changes, do set goals, but *be patient with yourself*. It's important to remember that there is a big difference between *knowing* something, and being able to *do* it. You can know and understand something within moments, but being able to do it, much less do it skillfully and easily, requires practice.

It's the same with any new skill set. For example, I've recently started taking golf lessons. As a new golfer, I've read plenty of articles and gotten lots of advice on how to hit the ball, and I can recite plenty of the key rules: Keep your head down, plant your feet, square your shoulders, follow through. I *know* what I'm *supposed* to do, but that doesn't keep me from shanking the ball off the tee and into the woods. The only way to get better is to set goals and continue to work on improvement, little by little.

Similarly, in learning to speak with greater confidence, authority, diplomacy, relatability, or compassion in a way that it will be recognized as such by the right people, it will also take time and practice. We all have someone who knows how to "push our buttons." Whenever we try to start a civil conversation with them, within a short period of time decorum goes right out the window. Don't expect to become best friends with the button-pushers in your life just because you've read this book. But *do* set goals for how you'd like the dynamic between the two of you to change. If you start a conversation well but then fall off the proverbial horse, get back up on it the next time and try again. Each time will get a little easier, and with each principle you apply, you'll be a step closer to where you want to be. Trust yourself, and trust the process.

You are now armed with the powerful insight of recognizing where you are standing in your own way, creating your own communication obstacles to success. You have a better understanding of why you might tend to be seen as too blunt, too passive, too fidgety, too monotonous, too unfocused, or too inflexible, and the effect that has on your ability to influence others positively. You also know what you need to do to fix it.

Change *is* possible. I've watched client after client go from feeling stuck and frustrated to feeling empowered, free, confident, and *happy*. Their relationships changed from merely collegial at best or perpetual stalemates at worst, to collaborative, mutually respectful, productive, and dynamic. Most importantly, in the eyes of others, their reputations changed from "a great colleague or employee but not leadership material," or "brilliant but hard to work with," to "a transformed leader." Once they started working on their communication skills as we've discussed, they were amazed at the doors that started to open in front of them.

So, what's the problem? How will you set about illuminating what is in your blind spot? What course of action will you take to correct it to improve your reputation, and have a greater, more positive impact?

- Maybe you need to get better at public speaking, media relations, or giving presentations.
- Maybe you need to be more diplomatic, less of the proverbial bull in the china shop.
- Maybe you need to muster up the courage and ability to address conflict head-on instead of always trying to run away from it.

- Maybe you're plagued with "the expert's curse" and need to learn to tell the *story* of your data and paint a picture for your audience instead of getting lost in the technical weeds.
- Or, maybe you just need to find the elusive balance between being relatable to others while still feeling authentically *you.*

One way or another, remember: *you and only you* have the ability to make this happen. I encourage you to continue on this journey to get out of your own way when you speak. Then watch how quickly you can establish your new reputation as a true leader worth following, and create a positive, lasting legacy.

You can start now to engage with your material, empower yourself, and energize your audiences. You now have all the tools you need to dig your way back out of the rabbit hole, into the daylight, where you can get a clear view of your vision and goals. Once you know what you want, you also have the tools necessary to inspire others to help you achieve it. Are you ready to discover the untapped powers of influence within you?

---

**Command the room.**
**Connect with the audience.**
**Close the deal.**

---

## VI. POINTS OF IMPACT

1. Using the tools in this book will help you learn to love engaging a wide variety of audiences, and that enthusiasm will empower your message even more.
2. The principles in this book are relevant in *any* context, regardless of your position or your relationship with the people with whom you're speaking.
3. Ask for feedback regularly and frequently. Honest feedback is one of the most valuable and necessary tools to identify your blind spot and measure change.

4. Be willing to step out of your comfort zone. This includes choosing people to ask for feedback, using video and audio recordings of yourself; and being willing to practice. Experiment with different approaches until it looks, sounds, and feels right to you, and lands with the desired effect.
5. You CAN do this.
6. Command the room. Connect with the audience. Close the deal.

## VII. BLIND SPOT CHALLENGE: PUTTING IT ALL TOGETHER

Redo your baseline video. Preparation suggestions:

- Change your content; change your wording, stories, or organization.
- Try to avoid fillers.
- Remember to breathe from the diaphragm and use your best voice, including "vocal periods," dropping your pitch so the listener can hear the ends of sentences.
- Use body language that reinforces your intended meaning and feeling, but does not distract. Use the P.E.G.S. checklist at the end of Chapter 5. It can also be found on the supplemental materials page at https://SpeakingToInfluence.com.

Then watch your video again, and using the Worksheets in the Appendix and on the supplemental materials page: https://SpeakingToInfluence.com (reference versions are included below), give yourself honest feedback about what was better, and what still needs work.

- Watch your video multiple times: First holistically, to see what your gut-level reaction is, as if you were the intended audience. Then go back and watch it at least three more times, each time looking at ONE of the Three Vs: the verbal, vocal, and visual channels. Refer back to the Blind Spot Challenges in Chapters 3, 4, and 5 for more specific guidelines.
- Write down progress, and set new goals until your message is clear and authentically delivered, and you are projecting your best leadership image.

Figure 6

## BASELINE RECORDING WORKSHEET

### STEP 1:
### Your Command Presence – Holistic Evaluation

Instructions: In the left column, list four qualities or characteristics you want people to recognize in you. Then watch your baseline video and score your video performance for how well each of those qualities shone through using the point scale in the right column. Make any notes as necessary to explain your score.

| Four Desired Qualities: Q1 - Q4 | Holistic Score: 0 – 1 – 2 (0 = missing, 1 = somewhat, 2 = clear) |
|---|---|
| Q1. | |
| Q2. | |
| Q3. | |
| Q4. | |

Figure 7

## BASELINE RECORDING WORKSHEET

### STEP 2:
### Your Command Presence – Deep-Dive Evaluation

Instructions: Take the four qualities (Q1 - Q4) listed in Step 1 and put them in the top row. Then watch your video again and look for each factor listed on the left. How did the factor influence the perception of each quality? You may want to watch the video more than once.

| Speech Factors | Command Presence Qualities and Scores Score each quality: 0 = missing, 1 = somewhat, 2 = clear | | | |
| --- | --- | --- | --- | --- |
| | Q1: | Q2: | Q3: | Q4: |
| Fillers | | | | |
| Organization | | | | |
| Run-on Sentences | | | | |
| Jargon/Vocabulary | | | | |
| Stories | | | | |
| Details (quantity, quality) | | | | |
| Speed, Pausing | | | | |
| Volume | | | | |
| Breath Support (no Vocal Fry) | | | | |
| Tonality (not Monotone/Up-speak) | | | | |
| Posture and Use of Space | | | | |
| Eye Contact/Movement, Brows | | | | |
| Gestures – Hand, Head, Other | | | | |
| Smile/Facial Expressions | | | | |

# APPENDIX

The Worksheets below are also available at https://SpeakingToInfluence.com

## BASELINE RECORDING WORKSHEET

### STEP 1:
### Your Command Presence – Holistic Evaluation

Instructions: In the left column, list four qualities or characteristics you want people to recognize in you. Then watch your baseline video and score your video performance for how well each of those qualities shone through using the point scale in the right column. Make any notes as necessary to explain your score.

| Four Desired Qualities: Q1 - Q4 | Holistic Score: 0 – 1 – 2 (0 = missing, 1 = somewhat, 2 = clear) |
|---|---|
| Q1. | |
| Q2. | |
| Q3. | |
| Q4. | |

# BASELINE RECORDING WORKSHEET

## STEP 2:
### Your Command Presence – Deep-Dive Evaluation

Instructions: Take the four qualities (Q1 - Q4) listed in Step 1 and put them in the top row. Then watch your video again and look for each factor listed on the left. How did the factor influence the perception of each quality? You may want to watch the video more than once.

| Speech Factors | Command Presence Qualities and Scores Score each quality: 0 = missing, 1 = somewhat, 2 = clear | | | |
| --- | --- | --- | --- | --- |
| | Q1: | Q2: | Q3: | Q4: |
| Fillers | | | | |
| Organization | | | | |
| Run-on Sentences | | | | |
| Jargon/Vocabulary | | | | |
| Stories | | | | |
| Details (quantity, quality) | | | | |
| Speed, Pausing | | | | |
| Volume | | | | |
| Breath Support (no Vocal Fry) | | | | |
| Tonality (not Monotone/Up-speak) | | | | |
| Posture and Use of Space | | | | |
| Eye Contact/Movement, Brows | | | | |
| Gestures – Hand, Head, Other | | | | |
| Smile/Facial Expressions | | | | |

## MASTERING THE MICROPHONE

There is nothing more frustrating than being unable to hear a speaker, particularly when I genuinely *want* to hear what they have to say. This happens with people who are speaking on panels, for interviews, in meetings, up on stage during a conference, in classrooms and lecture halls, and even in churches or other houses of worship. Even if the speaker has a microphone, it isn't clipped to them properly, or they have no idea how to hold it effectively. I catch myself leaning forward, craning my neck and even squinting my eyes just a bit, straining to hear what they say ... and getting annoyed in the process.

At that point, they have missed all three Cs of Vocal Executive Presence: They can't command the room or connect with the audience if nobody can hear them, and if they can't command and connect, then they certainly can't close the deal.

Assuming that you dislike sitting in that situation as well, and more importantly, that you don't want your audiences to associate such unpleasant and unsuccessful experiences with you, I want to talk to you about three different kinds of microphones (mics), and share a couple of quick do's and don'ts for using each kind comfortably and effectively.

The first is a lapel mic, or a lavalier ("lav") mic. A "lav mic" clips onto your collar, your tie, your shirt near a button, or your lapel. It has a wire that connects to a little box about the size of a pack of cigarettes that sits in your pocket or clips to your belt, and then transmits to the rest of the audio system. Although most venues will have a tech person who will get you hooked up, be sure to read through this section and double-check what they do because I find that they often overlook important details.

First, make sure that you know where you are sitting relative to the interviewer or moderator, if you're not speaking alone. The microphone should be clipped to the side near where they are sitting, because that's the direction you'll be looking for most of the time as you speak with them. You want to ensure that you're talking towards the microphone whenever possible for the clearest sound.

Second, an important rule of thumb is that nothing should make contact with the microphone head. Avoid wearing any necklaces or earrings that jingle and will make noise right next to the lav mic. Similarly, if you have long hair, either pull it back, or make sure the mic is placed somewhere your hair won't brush back and forth over it. If you are wearing a jacket, be sure the mic isn't clipped where it can get caught between your shirt and jacket. I'd even advise against tying a silk scarf around your neck when using a lav mic: if any of these things brush against the mic when you move, the noise coming through the speakers can sound like sandpaper.

Speaking of dress code, note that you'll need someplace to put the battery pack for a lav mic. If you're sitting down for an interview, it could simply sit on the chair behind you, but if you're planning to stand up and walk around as you speak, it will need to go into a pocket or clip to a waist band, belt, or pocket. Dresses can be problematic if they don't have a belt; you'll end up having to clip the battery pack to the back of your collar, which is particularly annoying and distracting, especially if the pack has a little antenna that keeps poking you in the back of the head!

There's another potentially embarrassing pitfall to avoid with lapel mics, particularly if event organizers hook you up a little while before you need to speak: Be sure that the power switch on the battery pack is turned *off* if you decide to visit the restroom! Trust me, that's a preview nobody wants to listen to, and probably not the fanfare you want to precede your grand entrance on stage. It makes you long for the days when the worst thing you had to worry about was whether or not you were walking in with toilet paper stuck to your heel.

The second kind of microphone you might use is a podium mic. Whether it's at a conference, a formal dinner or other company event, a fundraiser, or press conference, first and foremost, you *must* make sure that the microphone height is even with your mouth. For those of you who are on the short side, like me, don't let it aim at your forehead or even over your head. Remember that if you've got printed notes on the podium in front of you, you will naturally look down even further to read them, so bring the mic down to the appropriate height. Alternatively, if you are on the taller side—or simply speaking after someone who is shorter than you are—make sure you raise the mic angle so that it is not pointing at your chest.

Note: The rules for the podium mic also apply, for example, if you're sitting at a table on a panel. The mic stand might be on a table top rather than permanently attached to the podium, but the principles are the same. Be sure to move it in front of your mouth, especially if you are sharing the mic with another speaker, and lean into it each time it's your turn to speak.

Here's a quick geometry lesson for using podium mics: Besides adjusting it to the right height, when possible, you always want to have three things in a straight line: your mouth, the microphone, and the audience, in that order. If you're looking at the people who are right in front of you, and the microphone is right in front of your mouth, it should catch anything you say. But if you turn your head to the side, you don't want the microphone to be pointing at your ear. Your voice will suddenly sound softer and muffled.

Instead, if you are looking to the left, move your head and lean ever so slightly to the right, essentially pivoting around the microphone, so it is still directly between your mouth and the audience. That way, you're always aiming your sound right into the microphone for the best and most consistent sound quality.

One important question to ask your tech person ahead of time is if it is an *omni*-directional or *uni*-directional mic. An omnidirectional mic means it will pick up sound well from just about any direction. The microphone can be next to you, in front of you, above you, pointing in a slightly different direction, but it will still pick up whatever sound is around it. It is a bit more forgiving, if you haven't positioned the mic optimally.

However, more often than not, what you'll have is a unidirectional mic, which means it will only clearly pick up what sounds are spoken directly into it. To illustrate why this is critical, let's discuss the third kind of microphone, which is the dreaded handheld mic.

Most people hold a microphone in three very unproductive ways. The first is like an ice cream cone. They hold it relatively close to their mouth, but completely vertical, pointing up at the ceiling, often right under their chin. They end up speaking *across* the *top* of the microphone instead of *into* the microphone. If you're playing the jug in a bluegrass band, that might be a good strategy, but it's not for effective public speaking.

The second mistake is holding the microphone like a bouquet of flowers. It may start out in proper position or possibly like the "ice cream cone" as I just described, but over time, the arms relax and the microphone slides down further and further, until the speaker is holding it around chest- or even waist-level. Now they look more like a bridesmaid holding a bouquet of flowers than a keynote speaker or emcee. Unsurprisingly, the further down the mic is held, the less voice it picks up.

Taken a step further, the third common mistake when holding a hand-held mic is to unintentionally imitate a security guard with a flashlight, or an orchestra conductor with a baton. As many people are not used to having something in their hand when they talk, they gesticulate as usual, and the mic ends up moving all over the place without serving any real function.

If you know you will or even might have to use a handheld microphone, be sure to practice talking while holding a mic, or something similarly heavy, like a bottle of water or a meat tenderizer. One pound might not seem like much, but you'd be surprised how heavy it becomes when you have to hold it still for an extended period of time. It's important for you to get comfortable with the weight so your arm doesn't get too tired, and the microphone stays put in front of your mouth, which is where it belongs.

Whether it is omnidirectional or unidirectional, the ideal way to hold the microphone is directly in front of your face, pointing at your mouth as if you were playing a trumpet. That way your voice is going directly into the microphone where it can pick up your voice most effectively, and project the best quality sound to reinforce your best leadership image.

When you use your microphone effectively, you'll command the room, connect with your audience, and close the deal.

Have fun!

## "LISTENING TO INFLUENCE" STEPS

(Consider giving both/all participants a copy of these guidelines before or at the start of your conversation.)

1. Remind yourself: the goal is listening to *understand*, not listening to *win*. Seek to truly understand the other person's concerns, priorities, pressures, and needs. If both people successfully listen to understand each other, both people win.
2. Establish safety. Ensure the other person that there will be no retaliation if you don't like something they share. What matters most is getting to the real root of the problem.
3. Once you've established the purpose of the conversation, invite the other person to talk first.
4. Have paper and pens for each person to take notes while the other person is talking. Taking notes on computer can tempt people to secretly "multitask." Writing on paper ensures transparency, and can be scanned later if needed. Note-taking helps you to:
   a. Remember what the other person said
   b. Organize, revise, and prioritize thoughts before you share them
   c. Refrain from interrupting, since there's no concern that you'll forget what you wanted to say. Only interrupt to request immediately necessary clarification, or to gently guide tangents back on track.
5. Once they have shared their perspective, mirror back what you heard them say. Use reporting language, and avoid interpretation or judgment. Stay neutral in word choice, voice, and body language. Let the other person correct your understanding as necessary.
6. Acknowledge and validate as many of his or her points or feelings as possible.
7. Change roles. Ask the other person to take notes and listen to understand as you share some additional information.
8. Remind them to: (a) refrain from interrupting, (b) mirror using neutral reporting language, (c) ask them to acknowledge validity in something you've shared.
9. Repeat the process as necessary to reveal all crucial information to get to the best possible outcome while maintaining mutual respect and strengthening all relationships in the process.

# WORKS CITED

Burg, Bob, and John David Mann. *The Go-Giver: A Little Story About A Powerful Business Idea*. New York: Portfolio/Penguin, 2010. Print.

Cuddy, Amy. TEDGlobal Talk 2012: "Your Body Language May Shape Who You Are." https://www.ted.com/talks/amy_cuddy_your_body_language_shapes_who_you_are

*Ferris Bueller's Day Off*. Dir. John Hughes. Perf. Matthew Broderick. Paramount, 1986. Film.

Gladwell, Malcolm. *The Tipping Point: How Little Things Can Make a Big Difference*. New York: Back Bay Books, 2002. Print.

Goldsmith, Marshall. *What Got You Here Won't Get You There: How Successful People Become Even More Successful*. New York: Hyperion, 2007. Print.

Mehrabian, Albert, and Morton Wiener. "Decoding of Inconsistent Communications." *Journal of Personality and Social Psychology* 6.1 (1967): 109-114. Print.

*Mr. Holland's Opus*. Dir. Stephen Herek. Perf. Richard Dreyfuss, Glenne Headly, and Olympia Dukakis. Hollywood Pictures, 1996. Film.

Scannell, E., and J. Newstrom. *The Big Book of Presentation Games: Wake-Em-Up Tricks, Ice Breakers, & Other Fun Stuff*. New York: McGraw Hill, 1998. Print.

*Sex and the City*. Perf. Sarah Jessica Parker, Kim Cattrall, Kristin Davis, and Cynthia Nixon. Prod. Darren Star Productions, Home Box Office (HBO), and Sex and the City Productions, 1998-2004. Television.

Sinek, Simon. TEDxPuget Sound 2009 Talk: "How Great Leaders Inspire Action." https://www.ted.com/talks/simon_sinek_how_great_leaders_ inspire_action

--. *Start with Why: How Great Leaders Inspire Everyone to Take Action*. New York: Penguin Books, 2009. Print.

*The Wolf of Wall Street*. Dir. Martin Scorsese. Perf. Leonardo DiCaprio, Jonah Hill, and Margot Robbie. Paramount, 2013. Film.

CPSIA information can be obtained
at www.ICGtesting.com
Printed in the USA
LVHW052352110419
613930LV00009B/196